Love Mondays

James Raath

Clink Street

London | New York

Personal References

"As Chairman of 'The Parcel Company' 20 years ago I was privileged enough to have James direct my thoughts regarding the kind of culture I wished to establish in my then small business. Applying the principles I learnt from him, my business grew rapidly as most of my employees began to treat my business as if it were theirs - the results were spectacular. What was more rewarding to me than growth or profit however, was to see 'my people' completely engaged in our workplace, which for the majority of them led to deeply satisfying careers, personal growth and for a few to them 'leaving the nest' and starting out on their own. If investing in people not profit, is your heart, applying what you learn in 'Love Mondays' will see you successful in both"
Hugh Thöle - Entrepreneur

"James I have always enjoyed our sessions and have applied the many lessons that you have taught me and my teams with great results. I share your views that we are to include People in all aspects of our business and not just as deliverers of strategy. Everyone, where possible, must be part of the sanctioning of plans etc. and through that you will get buy-in as well as positive outcomes. Due to the environment that one creates in the work place everyone can be excited about Mondays and the week ahead. Once you create that environment and balance, the markets you play in will feel the culture from your business and want to deal with you. From there the battle is already half won."
Karl Bauermeister - CEO Sizwe Asset Finance (Pty) Ltd

"As a Business Advisor in South Africa, working with CEO's to grow and develop their business, I came to realise that the problem of getting genuine staff engagement in a company is the biggest threat to business, even bigger than a failing economy. I looked around for a solution and found James Raath. I came to England in December 2007 for a Training session and have worked with him ever since. His bravery in extreme adversity has inspired me. His book *Love Mondays* is a breakthrough and I believe it is every CEO's and business leader's handbook on how ordinary people

can accomplish the extraordinary in any business. By moving beyond staff engagement to embracing their unique ability and entrepreneurial drive, it offers leaders and staff a fresh and highly relevant approach to overcoming the challenges every business faces."
Dr Michael J Freestone. CPA. ABP FCIS. FCIBM. DBA (New York)

"I have worked with James in his consultancy over a number of years. His methodologies are pragmatic and effective, a blueprint for any CEO to harness that much sought-after but seldom-achieved commodity — staff initiative. Any business leader seeking to improve shareholder value will benefit from his book and its principles."
Ian Woodrow - On Digital Media

"There are two key take-aways from 'Love Mondays'. The first is that leaders already have the means to make better use of their greatest competitive advantage, their staff, without spending huge amounts of money or employing legions of consultants. The second is that employees have it within their power to take ownership of their role and make the most of it. If these occur in parallel, businesses can unleash the latent power of an engaged workforce and people can enjoy being at work. The appeal of this book is irresistible."
Harry Cruickshank – Interim Manager & Business Advisor

"In these times where technology plays an increasing role in business we often forget that the foundation of any good business is its *people*. It is of vital importance that we offer an opportunity for their development and also bring back the 'human touch' thus ensuring our people are in tune and aligned with the values and ethos of the organisation, and that every individual understands his/her role, contribution and responsibility for their own and their organisations success. The experiences and challenges faced by James Raath in business and personally will give him a unique insight and empathy to the benefit all stakeholders."
Jose de Almeida - General Manager SAV systems

Contents

Author's Note

I remember so clearly, thirty years ago, the excruciating disconnect I felt between the massive drive I had within me to express myself and excel in my career, and what was required of me in my job at that time as a product manager, particularly as I had stopped believing in the product I was selling. This was a real crisis for me and I was in a real dilemma. Should I stay or leave?

I left to join another company in a similar market, but soon found myself in a similar position. Was I the problem, was it the job, the company or my boss? As I look back, probably mostly me, but it made me look critically at all four, a process that changed the course of my life. I left to do my 'own thing' with only the most basic idea of what I was going to do and how I was going to do it. What followed were the most thrilling years of my life as I lived in a personal world of extraordinary opportunity and foolish blunders that put me onto a fast track programme of 'learn or go bust'. I learnt very quickly and also went bust... twice. However, in the process I learnt that *my* highest success hinged on me helping *customers* achieve their important goals by creating value that was available exclusively from me.

What I also learnt was that it took 'all of me' to *see* and *capture* the 'whole opportunity'. 'All of me' meant that I needed to be passionate about what I was doing. I needed a vision and purpose that fully engaged me that was beyond my need for money. The 'whole opportunity' was a 'marriage' between my customers' highest aspirations, and me expressing my highest talents and desires in meeting those aspirations for the financial reward I was seeking. The more I helped my customers achieve, the more I earned. I experienced this simple correlation time after time in the many projects and deals I was involved in.

Today, many businesses do not fulfil their potential. This book deals with two reasons for this. Firstly, there is still a widely held belief that profit is more important than the employees who generate it. Running a close second, is the myth that a company with a great product and strong management team, but with a workforce who do not share the company's vision, whose primary purpose is a monthly wage, will avoid obsolescence. According to Professor Richard Foster from Yale University, the average lifespan of a listed company today is just 15 years. I think that is tragic. We know that every business is gradually becoming redundant and will cease to exist *unless* it is able to create new relevant value for customers at a pace that exceeds its pace of obsolescence. Isn't this startling fact so important, that creating new value in a business should be everyone's priority? I think so.

Perhaps at a more fundamental level is the myth that integrity and morality are no longer as important as they used to be, or that the erosion of these forces for good have nothing to do with weak financial performance or our global financial crisis. I think they do. Because we reap everything that we sow, when we cross the lines between self-interest and selfishness, noble ambition and competitive envy – lines that that are sometimes so subtle we don't even notice them – we limit ourselves, constrain those we lead and deny our customers, ourselves and investors the potential value that could be created.

This book explores the building blocks that awaken entrepreneurial motive and purpose in employees, thereby safely bringing 'entrepreneurial life' to a company's plans in a way that transforms the business and impacts customers to want to buy more. It embraces a paradigm that redefines what can be achieved, where a leader's vision and motivation can be truly shared personally by everyone. It is a paradigm that replaces the constraining standards of conventional thinking with a set of 'higher rules', which produce a totally new standard of performance that, in turn, creates a totally new standard of 'customer spend' and cash flow.

It introduces an achievable standard that any organisation or team is capable of reaching. This standard which can be measured, is also the threshold that transforms 'job functions' into highly energising and fulfilling 'elite business missions', which transform ordinary profits into sustainable profit growth, enabling chief executives and their teams to achieve their highest strategic intent.

It is my hope that by reading this book, company leaders at all levels, and the people they lead, will see why they might be sitting on an invisible 'gold mine' of untapped opportunity and how, by embracing the principles in this book, they can *Love Mondays* as they work together to achieve a deep and long-lasting impact on both company results and their careers.

James Raath

Acknowledgements

Special thanks to my wife Robyn for her years of support, without which this book would most certainly not have been written. Special thanks also to my brother John for his valuable editing and advice, and to my many friends who did not allow me to give up. A special thank you to my good friend Dr Michael Freestone for his ongoing encouragement through the many years it took to complete this project, and acknowledgement to Coach Dan Sullivan, who first coined the terms *unique ability* and *unique teamwork*.

Introduction

How much of the 'grand vision' that permeates the mind of a business leader gets reduced to a 'budget' in the mind of managers, a 'task' in the mind of staff members, and an 'indifferent experience' for customers... deflecting revenue and profits to competitors?

I think this is a fair question to ask in the context of a book about the *personal impact* people bring to a business because it reflects the reality, at least in part, of many companies, even though they might be 'satisfied' with the level of their employee engagement. Losing sales and profits through hard fought competition is one thing, but losing today's sales and profits while everyone *'thinks they are doing a great job'*, when they could be doing so much better, means losing tomorrow's sales and profits too... without the faintest idea that it is happening.

Customers who should have spent money with a company spend it with their competitors, usually without a second thought, because they were denied any distinguishing value they were seeking for the money they were spending. And this is not just about the sales team. It is about *every* person in a company and *everything* they do, *every day*. It takes the 'whole person' to *see* and *capture* the 'whole opportunity' that is unique to a business. This *is* what energises the business strategy... nothing else does. The extent to which this is a living reality for every employee in every role in a business, and in every part of its distribution chain, every working day, determines *how much* of the *potential* value of that business, projected towards its customers, is actually *experienced* by them. What customers **experience today** will determine how much they **spend tomorrow**. This is what determines the pace of growth or decline of the business.

The scale of these daily losses and opportunities to every company and its investors cannot be read in its accounts, although they are most definitely reflected.

What is Personal Impact?

Personal impact is what employees bring to a business when their collective drive and talent propels it forward to new levels of performance that distinguish it in the minds of customers and competitors.

It occurs only when people reach beyond conventional skills, service levels and current experience by applying their unique ability, innovativeness and entrepreneurial engagement in executing a business's mission that they consider to be their own. This requires people to redefine the value they produce by combining their conventional skill set with two additional components that often lie dormant and unrecognized – their unique ability and entrepreneurial drive.

It is this powerful combination that is the source of a business's commercial impact, and the driving force behind that most elusive of goals... sustainable growth. While individuals who adopt this approach will make their own unique impact, its full benefit to a business is only felt when applied in a team context and ultimately throughout an organisation.

The theme of *personal impact* is therefore underpinned by five integrated and sequential concepts that need to be defined.
• Skill Set
• Unique Ability
• Entrepreneurial Drive

- Unique Teamwork
- Corporate Community

Skill Set is what usually defines a person's conventional value in the workplace. It is a combination of their acquired knowledge, experience and skill. On its own, a person's skill set usually does not add any unique value, but when applied in combination with that person's *unique ability* and *entrepreneurial drive* in the context of *unique teamwork*, a new world of opportunity opens to them.

Unique Ability is the ability to do things in a unique way or have a unique perspective. This ability is the result of the *special talent* that resides deep within every person that is often not recognised by them. When coupled with that person's skill set and ignited by their entrepreneurial drive, *personal impact* is produced that is unique to them and the business in which they are employed.

Entrepreneurial Drive is the motivation a person has to take charge of shaping their economic future by working to create their own unique impact on a business. This motivation is derived from the mind-set that personal opportunity and reward are entirely determined by how much their company and customers value what they do for them. For this reason, they are constantly alert to new opportunities to exceed the expectations of their company and customers, and constantly working to shape and refine their unique contribution.

Unique Teamwork occurs when a team works to create synergy from the unique ability of each team member, thereby leveraging *personal impact* to even greater value.

Corporate Community is the sense of belonging and shared purpose employees experience in a business that truly values people, and places a priority on their ability to deliver *personal impact*. It is the key to organisational synergy and sustainable growth.

Part 1

Challenging the Status Quo

Personal Impact Illustrated

Why you might be sitting on an invisible and largely untapped 'goldmine' of opportunity

The model below provides a visual illustration of three possible levels of employee engagement, only one of which enables employees to fulfil their commercial potential and therefore a company's growth potential. The other two either inhibit growth or actively obstruct it. Company earning power is therefore enhanced when the actions of employees are motivated by their entrepreneurial drive or constrained by their job mind-set. *Personal impact* is defined by where a job mind-set ends and entrepreneurial drive starts. Wherever an entitlement mind-set is encountered, growth is obstructed.

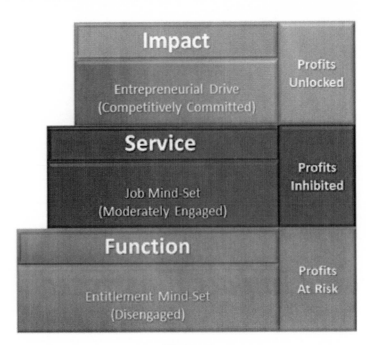

Figure 1

We will now illustrate the reality of the above model by exploring what happens in a fictitious company: Bailey's Logistics Plc. This will help us understand why, even when leaders work so hard on and in their companies, they do not do better. It will explain why, although companies have the necessary technical and management skills within their organisational structures, sales and profitability so often do not reach their potential. It will also explain why, when people in a business are *'alive'* with its vision, strategy and brand in a way that customers *'feel'* and are *'impacted'* by, more is spent on their products and services and less on their competitors. It will explain too, how *personal impact* is as applicable to internal 'customers' as it is to external paying customers and why nothing else has the power to distinguish a company in an over-crowded global market place, and why no matter how good the strategy and plans of a business are, it is only the dynamism of *personal impact* that can keep it from the swamp of mediocrity.

The problem is not one of effort, as people generally work very hard at what they do. The problem is the current paradigm that limits what companies and employees believe is possible. To challenge current thinking requires that we challenge current standards.

Defining the Function Zone

In the 'function' zone employees apply their skills to the job without any thought or effort to make a difference. They provide the minimum that is required of them to get the job done. This has nothing to do with the level of skill the person brings to the business and everything to do with the attitude of their engagement. A person who operates in the 'function' zone believes they are 'owed' a job and a living because it is their right. They are only interested in their pay cheque. They are often disgruntled with their employer and with life in general and have no 'spark'. Where this attitude exists there is no personal responsibility and no connection whatsoever between their work, customers and what the company is trying to achieve. This negative spirit, void of any purpose beyond earning a wage, is a poison that can spread and undermine the vision, mission and profitability of a business. Let's see how this plays out in Bailey's Logistics.

Applying the Function Zone to Bailey's Logistics Plc.

It's a typical day and Harry Jones, the regional sales manager, is behind in his preparations to pitch for new business from Eagle Star Foods, a national producer of breakfast cereals. Mary at the reception desk, still bearing the frown she left home with after an argument with her partner and problems getting the kids off to school, barely acknowledges his greeting.

What might not have mattered nine days out of ten mattered today, because in Mary's negative state of mind she did not bother to tell Harry Jones about the message she had put on his desk that Eagle Star Foods had phoned to say his presentation had been brought forward because the chief executive of Eagle Star Foods wanted to attend. Because Harry Jones was late, as he so often was these days, he decided not to go to his office, but to try to complete his preparations in a company meeting room. Of course had he received his message, he would have solicited the help of his boss Peter Drake, the national sales director, who normally only made himself available in situations of extreme importance.

While in the meeting room waiting for his coffee to cool, Harry Jones began to wonder why he was not that concerned about this sales pitch. He had brought in enough business in the five years he had been with the company, but recently mistakes, bad service and a looming strike by the operations department made him doubt the company's ability to meet new customer demands. He remembered the statement made by Burt Franklin the operations manager at last month's meeting, where he bemoaned the extra work load he and his team had to put up with. So Harry Jones decided to make things easy for himself and use an old presentation that did not feature the company's newest vehicle fleet or the client's new mission statement from their latest annual report.

Of course Harry Jones's arrival fifteen minutes 'early' was actually fifteen minutes late. Harry Jones's lateness was made worse by his ill preparedness. Eagle Star Foods might have overlooked these misgivings if they could find any real sense of personal belief by Harry Jones in what he was trying to sell. They did not. The presentation did not go well and Bailey's Logistics lost the opportunity to secure a five-year contract worth £250,000 a month.

Defining the Service Zone

The 'service' zone is where employees are moderately engaged in applying their skills and themselves to their job and the business, but with clear limits as to their willingness to proactively explore the full potential of their value. This is the zone in which the majority of employees operate in. They understand the rudiments of service, but there is a limit to how far they are prepared to go. Service is viewed as something they are paid to provide, rather than a heart-felt passion to provide excellence.

Employees who operate in the 'service' zone are often career minded but do not see their careers as a 'business'. If they did, they would do everything in their power to define, shape and deliver the unique value that would place them in the 'impact' zone. Personal responsibility would be total, not partial.

The concept of *service* is powerless today in differentiating a business in the eyes of customers because not only is it expected, it is also relatively easy to achieve and most companies do a reasonable job at providing it. Therefore many companies fail to achieve their true potential because achieving *good service* is the limit of their understanding of excellence. Failure to realise that the 'service' zone is no longer a competitive differentiator means that companies do not expect more from their employees. This is demonstrated as we apply this to the story of Bailey's Logistics.

Applying the Service Zone to Bailey's Logistics Plc.

It was not a typical day for Harry Jones, the regional sales manager, because he was about to pitch for new business from Eagle Star Foods, a national producer of breakfast cereals. He had worked on the relationship for months, and finally the day had come to make the presentation, which also contained Peter Drake the national sales director's valuable input. Mary at the reception desk was always good natured and could be relied upon to provide a good 'company face' to visitors, as well as take and manage messages for staff when required.

After greeting Harry Jones with a smile, she reminded him about the message she had put on his desk that Eagle Star Foods had phoned to say his presentation had been brought forward, because the chief executive of Eagle Star Foods wanted to attend. Harry Jones went immediately to the office of his boss Peter Drake, the national sales director, to ask him to accompany him to the presentation. Peter Drake gladly moved two previously arranged meetings to do this, but without any explanation to the people he had just cancelled meetings with. This was a mistake.

Had he explained to Burt Franklin, the operations manager, that the reason for postponing the meeting was to attend the Eagle Star Foods sales presentation, Burt Franklin would have told him of the latest customer satisfaction report he had just received that placed Bailey's Logistics in second place in industry ratings, up from sixth place as recorded in the previous report that Eagle Star Foods had a copy of.

Harry Jones, in the meantime, continued to practise his presentation, which did feature the company's newest vehicle fleet and the client's new mission statement from their latest annual report.

Harry Jones's experience and preparedness meant that the presentation to Eagle Star Foods went well and they were impressed with the offer. But not impressed enough. Bailey's Logistics did not win the opportunity to secure a five-year contract worth £250,000 a month.

Defining the Impact Zone

The 'impact' zone is where employees express their unique ability and entrepreneurial drive. This produces an entirely new level of sustainable income growth to a business as a result of an entirely new and measurable paradigm of human performance – people so motivated and determined to transform the future of a business, its customers and their career that they go beyond conventional skills, service and current experience to fully express their unique talent, innovativeness and entrepreneurial engagement in executing a business vision they regard as their own.

But can this level of commitment be achieved and if so, what will it take to do so? This book attempts to demystify what might seem unattainable, and make tangible what comes naturally to every street trader in the third world who has learnt to compete for a very real goal... staying alive economically. This is how it works in Bailey's Logistics as we relook at the story.

Applying the Impact Zone to Bailey's Logistics Plc.

These are the days Harry Jones, the regional sales manager lives for. He prepares and trains for days like these as if his future were completely dependent on them. It is days like this that everyone in Bailey's Logistics also waits for... and with bated breath. Everyone knows when and to whom a major sales presentation takes place. They also want to know how things have gone... before the team arrives back. They ensure news travels around the company... fast. Why? Because Bailey's Logistics values its people above everything; they are the heart of the business and customers know it. They also share in the company's financial success, earning regular cash bonuses and participating in its share scheme.

Today is a major sales presentation to Eagle Star Foods, a national producer of breakfast cereals. Harry Jones has worked on the relationship for months, and finally the day has come to make the presentation, which also contains Peter Drake the national sales director's valuable input. Mary is no ordinary receptionist. She is relied upon to collate and disseminate company news. She has already told Burt Franklin, the operations manager, that the presentation to Eagle Star Foods is scheduled for today. She has also placed on Harry Jones's desk a copy of the report just received from Burt Franklin that places Bailey's Logistics in second place in industry ratings, up from sixth place as recorded in the previous report that Eagle Star Foods now have.

After greeting Harry Jones with a big smile and a 'Go for it Harry' look, she reminds him about the message she has put on his desk that Eagle Star Foods had phoned to say his presentation has been brought forward because the chief executive of Eagle Star Foods wants to attend. This is just what Harry Jones was hoping for, and he goes immediately to the office of his boss Peter Drake, the national sales director, to ask him to accompany him to the presentation. Peter Drake responds with a grin that he has already cancelled his meetings and that he wants Burt Franklin to also attend... and present the new industry report to Eagle Star Foods.

The three of them get together to plan their revised presentation which not only features the company's newest vehicle fleet and the client's new mission statement from their latest annual report, but also Bailey's Logistics' new industry rating.

Eagle Star Foods can see the belief in Harry Jones's eyes that he has total confidence in Bailey's Logistics' commitment to the standards of excellence that he presents. This is backed up by the integrity of Burt Franklin, the man responsible for making it all happen, and the leadership of Peter Drake. Bailey's Logistics not only win the opportunity to secure a five-year contract worth £250,000 a month, but negotiate extra performance bonuses because Burt Franklin has uncovered some additional 'technically sensitive' needs they firmly believe they could meet which would help Eagle Star Foods' own performance. This is agreed.

That year not only do Bailey's Logistics Plc. post its best results to date, but every staff member earns their largest bonus. Needless to say, the industry rating report also has a new leader.

What can we learn from Bailey's Logistics and how they achieved what they did? Let's take a close look at Bob Jones, the CEO. Bob Jones clearly understood that the 'impact' zone draws a clear distinction between people who only make a *contribution* to a business and those who *impact* a business and its profits. He also understood that when the qualities that define the 'impact' zone are fully developed in a business, any goal becomes achievable, but when ignored, mediocrity becomes inevitable – possibly even stagnation and economic obsolescence. Bob Jones displayed three crucial leadership qualities.

1. He realised that every person in his organisation either created or inhibited customer-spend... there was no neutral ground.

2. He saw potential value in people beyond their current skill and experience.

3. He allowed current engagement and profitability paradigms to be challenged and replaced by the higher standard of *personal impact*.

Every employee was encouraged to measure their own performance using a *Personal Impact Index* tool and given a mandate to define *where* and *how* impact could be created and added to their role. Figure 2 below shows the average score for the company.

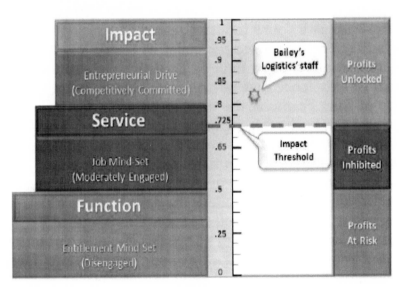

Figure 2

In addition to the average score for the company, the tool analysed five additional measures for Bob, which helped explain why such a high score was achieved. These are explained below. This encouraged Bob to continue with his current strategy of finding investors to aid the growth he knew he could achieve. The high impact score in his company gave Bob confidence in offering investors a high likelihood of good future performance providing *Higher Returns at Lower Risk,* as opposed to a low impact score that would indicate *Lower Returns at Higher Risk.*

Leadership

Bob understood that there was an umbilical cord between his company's strategic intent and its operational reality. This umbilical cord was how well his company vision and strategy was 'lived' by his leaders at all levels and how well it was embedded in the hearts and minds of his employees who had to execute it. This was also Bob's definition of leadership.

Entrepreneurial Drive

Bob knew if his leaders and their teams had the motivation to reach beyond their current experience, and were determined enough to impact the business's growth in a unique way, this would be demonstrated by their taking ownership of the new opportunities that they had taken the initiative to recognise. Not just in new sales, but also in small focused opportunities, captured every day by every staff member, that he knew would add up to the Big Sale.

Risk and Reward

Bob's bonus and share scheme worked because his people believed in what they were achieving, and were prepared to demonstrate this by sharing in the risks and rewards of poor or outstanding performance.

Innovation

Innovation came naturally to Bob's business as employees worked together to drive value up and costs down. This produced new saleable value and new 'bankable' efficiencies that far exceeded the bonuses that were paid.

Focus on Customers

Focus on customers came naturally because everyone shared in the philosophy that maximising impact on customers would maximise business results, and this was an integral part of how everyone treated everyone else in the company.

Dead or Alive?

Every person in an organisation either lifts or inhibits profitability... there is no neutral ground

At either end of the engagement spectrum, employees are a company's greatest asset or its worst nightmare; this leaves the bulk of employees in the seemingly innocuous middle category, found at all levels in an organisation, who are simply 'getting on with their jobs'. It is easy to assume that this is a satisfactory state of affairs because this large group of people are at least productive in carrying an important work load. But could it be that it is precisely their 'ordinariness' that is inhibiting their own and the business's growth? What would happen if the concept of 'work load' was replaced by 'opportunity', and everyday 'tasks' were transformed into important 'contributions' to make a real difference to a mission everyone understood and enthusiastically believed in? How would this affect company results?

This is the context in which a business is either 'alive' or 'dead'. It is 'alive' only when the chief executive's vision and purpose for the company is understood and enthusiastically embraced by everyone at every level, and everyone understands how, in the context of their role, they can make a unique contribution to making it happen. Work would then cease to be a grind for many, and become a thrilling challenge of shaping and building a company everyone is truly proud to be part of. However, a business is 'dead' or 'dying' when this level of enthusiasm and engagement does not exist. Mediocrity secretes its poison, and decline, however slow, inevitably sets in because 'ordinariness' does not embrace vision or challenge – it avoids them. Underneath the guise of 'ordinariness' is the knowledge that growth must always be 'fought for' and this requires effort, sometimes extraordinary effort and even risk, a price people who are not 'alive' with vision and purpose are not prepared to pay. A company's highest intentions and plans always require a noble and prolonged effort to overcome all kinds of obstacles, but this cannot be achieved by people void of vision, purpose and risk.

How often do we meet a CEO or business owner who is fully satisfied that their business is reaching its highest potential? How often do we meet people who find their work so completely fulfilling and energising that they can hardly wait for Monday morning? And how often do we meet people whose spectacular experience as a customer prompted them to share it with family and friends? Not that often.

Does this not suggest that sometimes, perhaps more often than we are prepared to admit, business leaders simply accept the limitations imposed on their plans by the prevailing standards of 'ordinary' human performance that produce 'ordinary' financial returns? What might happen to these standards if employees no longer worked just to earn a living but were instead motivated by a bigger purpose that, when achieved, would take care of their need for income and much more?

This opportunity and purpose at a personal level is what transforms the nature of work and what can be accomplished in a business. It transforms each 'job' into a 'business'; 'work' into 'opportunity'; 'company customers' into 'personal customers'; and 'moderately engaged employees' into 'committed company partners'.

Company Growth requires Personal Growth

Nothing can change in a company until its people change. It

24

seems logical to conclude that because *personal impact* is a uniquely human characteristic, and because it is often absent at many levels in a business, that company growth requires a specific kind of personal growth first. Most employees would agree that personal growth, together with achievement and expanding choices through increased income, are some of the more important rewards they seek from their work life. Although everyone would know exactly what they would do with the extra cash if they earned it, few employees are able to define and link the type of personal growth necessary to boost their commercial value to the level of *personal impact*, which would in turn result in boosted income.

It is the purpose of this book to present the life changing principles of *Unique Ability, Entrepreneurial Drive, Unique Teamwork* and *Corporate Community* that empower people and teams to be the primary force that brings life to business plans and new impetus to business growth. All this becomes possible when personal goals are linked to business goals, and business goals are measured by a standard of impact that always produces rewards to match.

One often hears a company head say, *"Our people are our single most important asset"*, but how often is that in fact a reality? William Rogers, CEO of UKRD Group, a multi-media company operating throughout the United Kingdom, explains how this is true for his company. *"It's critical that our business should focus equally as much upon its people as anything else, for they then drive all those other elements of the business. We not only develop the professional skills of our managers but also their personal skills and attributes too. It's critical that there is a real balance in terms of the growth of the personal as well as the professional sides of our managers. We believe passionately in developing both the personal and professional attributes of our managers and invest heavily in doing just that. We also encourage everyone in our organisation to develop themselves as people outside of work and allocate an amount of money each year so that any member of our team, at any level, can go off and do something of interest to them personally in terms of a skillset or hobby. As long as it's going to improve them as people, we'll pay the grant."*

In another example, Liberty Life, a highly successful financial services company in South Africa, had a particular challenge not uncommon to many companies. Employees needed to be re-aligned to the business and its customers during a difficult period of restructure introduced by the CEO as part of a revitalising project. To assist in this process, my company was asked to provide training to their teams on the principles of *personal impact*. The concepts, although new to many of their employees, helped them to adapt successfully to the changes they faced, and embrace their new opportunities.

Claudie Herman, a team leader, had this to say about how different the training was and the effect it had on her: *"It was like childbirth, you cannot really explain it, you need to experience it."*

A colleague, Hasinah Govindjee, also a team leader, expressed how the principles impacted him personally and his team: *"It was a huge learning experience for me personally, and for my team."*

Strategy, People and Profits

Between a strategic plan and the next set of financial results lies a defining chasm... its execution

A note to Chief Executives

Many months of hard work have been invested in your plan and strategy. The stakes are high. You know your business well, you have unstoppable belief in your product, your plan and the goals you have set – but like a professional sports coach you will be relying on your team, not just to perform well together, but also to deliver results against competitive odds. Because there is only so much that you can do, you will have to leave the rest to your team and organisation. So here is the pivotal question that must be answered:

"What do your vision, strategy and plan mean to your team and organisation who must execute it?"

- Do *they* see a compelling opportunity?
- Will its success enhance *their* future?
- Does it require *everyone* to raise the level of their contribution?
- Is every team inspired and supported by a strong leader?

In my experience there is often a significant gap between a chief executive's vision of a business's potential, and the reality reflected in the results produced by the organisation. We can either accept this discrepancy as normal, or we can challenge our paradigm of what is possible. Many strategies only document the *'what'* and *'how'* of a business but do not contain the critical ingredient required to drive its execution. What a chief executive would ideally want from their organisation is often hindered by how people in the organisation view themselves and the company's goals, how aligned they are to these goals, and what they are prepared to do to achieve them. Without a clear *'why'* for the people tasked with its execution, performance and profits are left at the mercy of employees' motivation, understanding and application which, unless it is boosted by the potency of *personal impact*, will be limited to just 'doing their job' and will be far short of what is possible, in spite of 'acceptable' leadership.

The omission of a strategic *'why'* affects strategy execution at all levels. Only when there is a *convergence* of motivation, understanding and application throughout an organisation will employees take on a chief executive's vision as their own and a chief executive's goals as their own. Any *divergence* of motivation, understanding and application however small, will always undermine what a chief executive is trying to achieve.

When the strategy includes a clear *'why'* for the people who must execute it, the convergence of motivation, understanding and application produces the unstoppable drive that makes the dream happen. People have within them a deep-seated desire for meaning and fulfilment and an amazing capacity to apply themselves to company challenges... when these challenges are personal. So, when employees truly share in a company's vision, are fully appreciated in demonstrable ways *and* incentivised well for performance, they will be inspired to deliver their very best. Then, anything becomes possible in a business.

Strategy is filtered through three stages, each stage affecting the next and as a result, strengthening or weakening strategy execution and profits.

The Motivation Filter

The first filter is the motivation filter. It is the most critical of the three because everything hinges on it, but it is also the most ignored aspect of strategy execution, possibly because it is not always well understood. The motivation filter does one of two things within people and within a business. When motivation is high, it stretches peoples' desire and ability, *empowering them to execute the strategy* thereby achieving business objectives. But when motivation is low, desire is weakened and ability hindered, thereby *diluting execution of the strategy* and damaging growth and reducing profitability.

The Understanding Filter

When motivation is strong, employees are prepared to stretch their minds to understand not just what is required of them, but what is possible to achieve collectively. The understanding filter either opens or shuts peoples' minds to the 'how' of achieving the new goals a strategy sets out to achieve. New goals and new challenges demand higher levels of understanding and new levels of ingenuity. This has to do with more than just verbal consent to ambitious plans. It has to do with people really *believing* in the opportunity they are engaged in and *wanting* to make it happen. So, where motivation is high objectives become personal, believable *and* well understood, but, when motivation is low, objectives are never personal, seldom fully understood and seldom fully accomplished.

The Application Filter

The application filter is about much more than just accuracy and commitment in getting the job done – it is about whether every person in the organisation or team is motivated and working hard to *improve* yesterday's performance, or whether they are just *repeating* it. It is the extent of this defining truth that determines whether a business's strategy is being executed effectively or not, and how quickly that business grows, stagnates or shrinks.

A Critical Problem

Many executives, entrepreneurs and team leaders have a critical 'Blind Spot' because they do not have the means to accurately measure:

1. The effect strategy filters have on the execution of their strategy.

2. The impact of this on customer-spend.

3. Their organisation's true capacity to create new value for the business.

As a result, many companies do not see the underlying problems that inhibit effective strategy execution, or the growth potential they are capable of – they simply settle for what they believe is the norm, the cost of which is often staggering. It is a well-researched fact that on average only about 20% of employees are competitively engaged (the impact zone), 60% are passively engaged (the service zone), while about 20% are actively disengaged (the function zone).

Relying on people to execute a strategy who do not share the belief, vision or passion for the business will always massively dilute potential sales and profits, while also diverting valuable time and resources to manage mediocre performance. Many leaders will argue that they have taken extensive measures to communicate their company's strategy and plans to their organisation or team. However, communication is much more than mental assent to what is required. What really matters is, *"What does it mean to the people who must execute it?"* Do they have an *unstoppable belief* and *desire to perform* fuelled by the deep pleasure of 'ownership'; uniqueness; confidence; passion; purpose; self-expression; achievement and reward? If they do not see the strategy as *their* greatest opportunity – it probably won't be the company's either.

The Solution

The solution is to create a culture supported by an effective measurement tool that empowers employees at all levels to take full responsibility for diagnosing and correcting their *own* performance short-comings, and to aid their own pursuit of success. Only when this is achieved will people become partners and custodians of the business's *vision, opportunity* and *plan,* seeking to manage themselves, while directing all their energy towards accomplishing the corporate task. This is how the gap between strategic intent and operational reality is closed.

William Rogers, CEO of UKRD Group, shared how he achieved such high employee engagement that his company was ranked number 1 in the UK 100 Best Mid Companies 2014 to work for. *"Employee engagement needs to be real and meaningful. Authority and autonomy are critical factors in delivering genuine engagement and simply paying lip service to it does not cut it. When managers at any level know they can make a decision and the results will be theirs to work through and ultimately witness; that's real engagement. It's important to ensure that you have open lines of communication where team members at whatever level can speak openly but fairly about any issue within the company to anyone at any level and know they will be listened to, that's real engagement. When ideas from whatever quarter are welcomed and encouraged and then properly looked at and responded to, that's real engagement. You know its real when you see it and you certainly know when it's fake too."*

Winners and Losers

Winners take more market share and profits – losers take less

We conclude Part 1 by asking: *"Why is it that the most successful companies, even in times of recession, are still the least satisfied with their results, becoming even more determined to do better, while others languish in the sea of mediocrity?"* Is the answer that 'belief' and the 'desire to excel' permeate the hearts and minds of employees in successful companies, while not in mediocre companies? If so, what is it that successful companies do or avoid, that mediocre companies ignore?

Underlying a carefully crafted strategy and business plan is a philosophy of doing business that believes that sustainable profit growth can only be achieved when there is a reciprocal relationship between a company and its employees to the extent that:

1. The company does not see its employees as merely a *resource* in the pursuit of profit, but the *reason* the company is able to generate profit.

2. Employees willingly align themselves to the business as partners and custodians of its *vision, opportunity* and *plan*, seeking to enhance their own performance and opportunity, by achieving goals that are significantly beyond their current experience, thereby accomplishing sustainable growth.

This is the difference between winning companies and losing companies. Winners take more market share and profits – losers take less.

Beneath Momentum

Financial results lag the causal reality in a business by anything between twelve and twenty four months, the general rule being the larger the company, the longer the lag. Mostly it takes many months before the current actions of people are reflected in the financial results, and when they are and changes are introduced, an equally long time for the changes to be reflected in future financial results. Without an early warning signal of impending problems or the confirmation that all is well, this could be a two to three year cycle at the cost of much lost ground and profitability.

As vital as financial results are for their intended use in business, they always produce a historical financial picture of what has happened (even six months is a long time in some businesses), but are of no value in understanding the strength or weakness of the *personal impact* of the people in the business that produce the results.

The Deception of Momentum

Momentum is every business leader's objective, and when things are rolling along well it is tempting to think it could never change. Momentum does that for us. It can lull us into thinking that we have finally 'got it right' and that all is well while actually hiding a dangerous turn for the worse that will not be identified before it has done the damage.

From bitter experience, leaders know that a business is never static but always growing or shrinking. So, what is needed is an early warning measure of whether momentum is sustainable or not, providing an understanding of the *'why'* that drives strategy execution. A tool is also needed to either correct problems early or reinforce the power of existing momentum.

Shifting Sand or Bedrock

When employees don't care deeply about the business they work in and leaders are not aware of how this is impacting customers and internal effectiveness, strategy and profitability are at serious risk without realising it. The reality is that in spite of a great vision and winning strategy, a business could be on shifting sand—without the chief executive realising it.

When the people who work in a business are competitively committed and their future linked to its risks and rewards they will really care, not just about their job and pay cheque, but about the company's future too, and because they are closest to the coal face, they become the 'ears and eyes' of what is really happening on the ground long before it is reflected in the financial results and their pay cheques. This, together with the vision and strategic plan, forms the bedrock of a successful business.

Taking the Shackles Off

Empirical data from research conducted on many companies indicate that CEO's and team leaders often feel 'trapped' in the gap between their strategic *intent* and the operational *reality* that is actually achieved. On the other hand, companies that 'raise the bar' of performance through a culture of entrepreneurial dynamism stretch employee capabilities and then reward them for going beyond 'yesterday's' performance. This desire within employees to perform at their highest levels can only be inspired – never forced.

I believe every company is sitting on an invisible and untapped 'goldmine' of new opportunity. It is invisible because the source of this new opportunity resides in the hearts and minds of employees. It is untapped because although many companies desire a culture in which this high level of commitment and performance can be embraced and activated, they do not have the necessary tool to do so. Such a tool is introduced at the end of the book.

For leaders with a big view of what is possible for their business through their people, Part 2 *Crossing the Great Divide* introduces new paradigms to bridge current experience to new standards.

Questions to consider

• How much of the 'grand vision' that permeates your mind as a business leader gets reduced to a 'budget' in the mind of managers, a 'task' in the mind of staff members, and an 'indifferent experience' for customers... deflecting revenue and profits to your competitors?

• What do your vision, strategy and plan really mean to your team and organisation who must execute it?

• Do employees willingly align themselves to your business as partners and custodians of its *vision, opportunity* and *plan*, seeking to enhance their own performance and opportunity, by achieving goals that are significantly beyond their current experience in order to achieve sustainable business growth?

Part 2

Crossing the Great Divide

Money, People & Business

A business will achieve its highest sustainable success when people are its primary focus instead of money because people (customers and employees) are the source and generators of its income

Could it be that an obsession to create wealth is the very thing that holds companies back from achieving their potential, because it blurs the thinking regarding where the focus should be? Is it possible that in many cases we have our priorities the wrong way around, having become so entrenched in the way we think and do things, that we overlook the obvious? To try to answer these questions, we will look at the relationship between money, people and business more closely to help us take stock of where we might be and why we could potentially be doing so much better.

Many businesses suffer from various degrees of 'commercial fatigue' – *the inability to respond swiftly enough to internal problems and the external opportunities that keep that business growing...because employees have simply run out of steam.* At best this is debilitating to a business, at worst it can be fatal. But 'commercial fatigue' will not be recognised until the real problem is identified. 'Commercial fatigue' is a symptom of a deeper problem which has its root in a value system where making money is more important than the people who make it happen – employees who generate saleable value and the customers who pay for it. This value system, which ultimately undermines a business's success and sustainability, blinds business leaders to the potential their employees have to truly impact customers and company revenue streams. The effects of 'commercial fatigue' can be observed at any level in a business where employees are unable to deliver their best work because of the relentless pressure to cope with increasing workloads and reduced staff levels. As a result they, and the business, are forced into survival mode.

The Natural Order of Income Generation

There is a natural order to generating income in a business, which is as natural as a stream of water finding the path of least resistance as it flows down a mountainside to a pond below – your business. Money flows naturally toward value that fills a need. After identifying need and then creating and delivering value to fill the need, money will flow as a result.

If we view business using this simple analogy, then to increase income and profit we must do two things. Firstly, we must increase the gradient of the flow of cash to our business by raising the value we offer for the money flow we are targeting, and secondly, we must increase the efficiency by which our value is delivered. This reduces resistance to the flow of money we have targeted caused by our own shortcomings. If this analogy holds true, then the *personal impact* of employees is an important key to combating competition and increasing the flow of money to your business.

Purpose in Business

If people are asked, "What is the purpose of business?" many would automatically respond with the answer, "To make money." But is the profitability of a business its goal or its purpose, and what is the difference? Let's take a closer look. Purpose connects a business to the source of its revenue... its customers. It defines the reason for a business's existence and the reason its customers buy from it. A business's purpose is expressed in the design, marketing and delivery of what it sells. Purpose is 'outward looking' defined by customer needs, while goals are 'inward looking' defined by the needs of the business. Both are necessary, but achieving the goal of making money comes only as a result of a primary focus on the purpose of the business, and the priority of fulfilling that purpose. When the purpose of a business becomes confused with its goal of making money, then the 'umbilical cord' to the source of its revenue is damaged, creating resistance to the 'natural' flow of income.

Having a stated corporate purpose is not enough to achieve the goal of profitability. To ensure that a business directs its focus and activity towards its customers, its purpose must be shared meaningfully by the people who work in it. It is this same purpose that must drive employees' careers. Purpose gives a goal meaning, thereby providing the human impetus necessary to achieve it. A goal without any underlying purpose has no meaning to the people who are required to achieve it, thereby disengaging them from it. Purpose is that uniquely human characteristic that dictates our level of engagement in achieving a goal because it connects with, and satisfies, our deep need to experience motivation and meaning in the work we do.

Therefore, ambitious profit goals can only be achieved when there is a high level of engagement of people, enabled and sustained by a high sense of shared purpose. Purpose provides a business with its long term sustainable drive to continue to achieve and grow, while at the same time enabling its profit goals, which are short-lived, to also be achieved.

People and Money

The value of money is diminishing every day as inflation takes its toll. If not invested, its value would eventually become meaningless. When people invest their money, many believe they are *"Making their money work for them so it can grow"*. But is this strictly true? Others believe that *"Money makes money"*. It does not – and it cannot multiply on its own. It never has and never will.

What is money? It is simply the currency people attach to the economic value added by people to the products and services we want to sell or buy. The more value people add to a product or service the more expensive and rarer it becomes, and therefore the more money is needed to buy it. With increased value comes increased pricing and increased income (money)… in that order. It is the process of people adding value that determines how money is generated, whether we purchase an item in a shop, do our work for our employer, mine diamonds or sell a company to investors. This applies to individual income, business income or national income. People are always the source of added value, value that must be first created before money can be generated. It is people whose ideas and ingenuity are converted into products and services, who create saleable value for customers and profit for investors. So what is more important to a business, its people or its money?

If we were to ask investors this question, many might instinctively choose money because it is their money which is at stake. However the wise entrepreneur, who has both a financial and intellectual investment in a business, asks a different question. The question is this. *"What is more important to my* <u>*customers*</u>*, my people or my money?"*

The entrepreneur knows that from a customer's point of view it is people who create, deliver and maintain the value that they exchange money for.

Pursuing Customers not Money

Motive is critical. A business either pursues customers or money. Pursuing customers is demonstrated by how much personal attention a business gives to engaging with them and the response of customers to this, by wanting to share their current and future needs with that business. The more intimately we know our customers, the more we learn about their needs. Customers happily spend more money with businesses that truly care about them and object to spending any at all with businesses that don't. Pursuing only money (an easy distraction) cannot be masked by 'clever' marketing platitudes. It is short-sighted and deprives a business of discovering and owning the best opportunities to generate the most sustainable income. Customers know this too, and are highly sensitive to when interest in their needs is real and heart-felt and when it is not.

Tristan Hunkin, Group Head of News at UKRD, shared what he believed his customers expect. *"They expect a company that they can trust, that is on their side and which wants to help them grow their business, rather than to make a quick buck at their expense. Each of our radio stations is at the heart of the communities that they serve, with locally based presenters and journalists – rather than content delivered remotely from hubs many miles away from their audience. That means that each of our teams is able to work to make a difference to the area that they serve – and to help change people's lives."*

Getting it Wrong

I believe there are still many companies whose paradigm of money, people and business is represented by Figure 3 below. It is a subconscious paradigm that affects all operations, even though lip service might be given to the importance of customers and employees. This apparently 'normal' situation hides the alarming truth that because money is actually the business's purpose, its source of *personal impact* (employees) and its source of revenue flow (customers) become secondary to the purpose of making money. When this happens the business loses its distinction and ability to compete with the best.

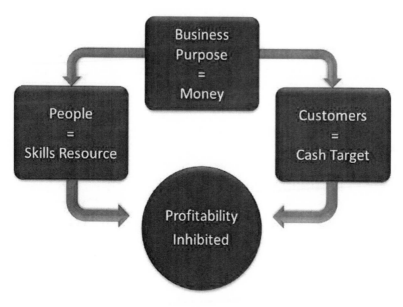

Figure 3

This has serious implications for everyone in the value chain; investors, customers, employees and society. What also happens when 'money rules' is that the noble principles of integrity are often ignored, thereby allowing greed to take root. This can lead to dishonest business decisions and an atmosphere of competing interests. No enterprise can maintain a competitive edge in such an environment.

When a business is regarded only as a source for profit for its owners, or bonuses for its management team, its purpose and potential for growth are easily lost. Employees regarded only as a skills resource have limited engagement in their work and even less engagement in the success of the business. When people are hired only *for* their skills that is all the company will get from them. But when they are hired *as people*, the company gets not just their skills, but their initiative, innovation and passion.

When a business is regarded only as a source for profit, customers are targeted only for their cash and any meaningful feedback they could provide about their needs and the business's performance is lost. Companies often try to hide the fact that money is their primary purpose through cheesy advertising slogans, but customers are not easily fooled.

Doing it Right

When a business defines its purpose in terms of meeting customer needs instead of making money (see figure 4 below) then the creation of saleable value to customers becomes the business's primary activity. *Personal impact* is recognised as the means to achieve this and is encouraged and incentivised. Employees, inspired by the vision and opportunities presented to them, become highly creative, productive and fulfilled by 'partnering' with the business and its customers. The result is that new wealth is created and investors, leaders, staff, customers and society are all positively impacted.

The greater the level of meaning derived by people from their work, the more they will contribute to the process of wealth creation. When the 'whole person' is engaged in the vision and mission of growing a business, and this happens in a collective way in an organisation, then the 'whole opportunity' available to the business can be seen and captured.

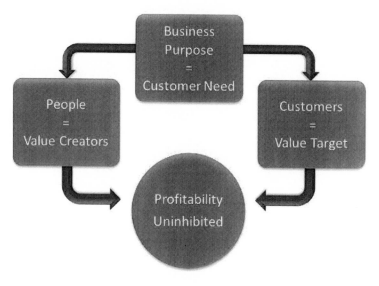

Figure 4

Importance of Money

The importance of money is not diminished but enhanced by this understanding of the role of people in a business. When people see the financial impact of their own efforts and realise what it took to achieve, they will acquire a new appreciation of the value of money. They will control money more carefully, put it to use more wisely and protect it as if it were their own.

Investors, who understand this approach to business, will seek to put their capital to work in businesses that have an ethical entrepreneurial culture embedded in the organisation. They will have peace of mind that these businesses employ people who also understand the true value of money and who share in the risks and rewards of its growth.

Investors, who seek evidence of entrepreneurial drive only in the senior management team, and not in the culture of the organisation itself, limit their investment returns to conventional levels. Those who seek this evidence more broadly in an organisation have access to opportunities for far greater returns.

Laws of Noble Enterprise

Principles that ignite and align performance, purpose and ethics to create a benchmark in business that makes financial success inevitable

Businesses that are careful about protecting their revenue streams by not allowing their customer-orientated *purpose* to be 'hijacked' by their *goal* of making money, will also be careful to create a culture in which these values are protected. This requires a performance charter as well as a moral charter that people can aspire to which must be modelled by the leadership that supports it.

When it comes to the high stakes that exist in business and the complexities of human relationships on which so much depends, a culture of excellence supported by a moral charter, creates a unifying bond across the different backgrounds of employees, and a common buffer against problems that emerge from our human shortcomings. The *Laws of Noble Enterprise* are universal principles that inspire and motivate people at all levels in a business to work together for a purpose that is bigger than their own need for income.

These principles also empower people to seek their highest opportunities for advancement and fulfilment, thereby freeing them to participate at new levels and achieve what was previously unthinkable. They help leaders and their teams to define their difference and maximise their impact by igniting and aligning purpose, ethics and performance to create a benchmark that makes financial success inevitable.

The Laws of Noble Enterprise are a composite of entrepreneurial, spiritual and moral laws (see figure 5 below), that provide the foundation for the unique ability, entrepreneurial drive, unique teamwork and corporate community that empower organisations to reach their highest potential. Entrepreneurial endeavour is never hindered by spiritual and moral considerations – it is set free!

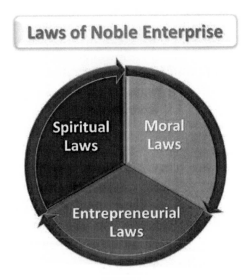

Figure 5

Entrepreneurial Laws

Entrepreneurial laws ensure the highest expression of competitive drive and creative behaviour within people, in both visualising and building sustainable economic opportunity. To some people these laws come more naturally, but for most of us they must be learnt; not as text book theory but as experiential principles that come to our aid to help us survive, and then thrive, when faced with the unyielding challenge of marketplace competition. Most employees do not understand what this means until they are introduced to the 'sharp end' of a business where their own financial reward is, at least in part, determined by the degree to which their own 'customers' value what they do for them.

Each law, when internalised, brings a unique dynamism and impact to the daily work life of a person and what they are able to achieve. Then, when each law is adopted and practised in the context of a team, that dynamism is further leveraged to forge a unique impact on a business. When adopted throughout an organisation, it makes any corporate goal achievable.

Spiritual Laws

Spiritual laws are universal laws of cause and effect that govern the outcomes of human behaviour. Every thought or expression of human behaviour has a consequence, good or bad, dictated by spiritual laws. This includes the goals we set, our performance, our creativity, our persistence, how we deal with success and setbacks and, of course, our relationships. Our ultimate success or failure is dictated by these unseen and unchanging spiritual laws that are real and that we have no control over. If we choose to apply them we will enjoy the enormous benefits they bring to us, but if we choose to ignore them we will not be able to ignore the results they inevitably produce in our lives.

Moral Laws

We do not live in a moral void. We all have a sense of what is right and wrong. Moral laws are designed to give us insight into the kind of behaviour that will result in positive consequences. By obeying moral laws we ensure that the spiritual laws work for us, not against us. Morality is something we can respond to that gives us a measure of control over the outcomes of our choices and behaviour.

*

The idea that our actions, and therefore the resultant outcomes that we do see, are influenced by unseen spiritual and moral laws is not new. Neither is this an idea that is only understood by philosophers, mystics and religious people of different persuasions. It is simply a fact of life, and is embedded in our experience (whether we recognise it or not) as permanently as the laws that dictate our physical world such as gravity, or buoyancy.

By illustration: a sharp word to a colleague or employee will usually result in that person feeling offended, while a kind gesture to someone has the opposite effect. These are simply spiritual and moral laws in action.

Science seeks to understand truth by studying the relationship between 'cause' and 'effect' in our physical world. For example, the unchanging laws of physics that control and protect our physical universe have formed the basis of every successful engineering or scientific invention. Any neglect or attempt to ignore these laws by us will be painful, costly and may even result in our demise. Put simply, only by understanding and mastering our application of the laws of physics are we able to master our physical universe. The same principle is applied to our spiritual world.

As spiritual and moral beings, we need to master the unchanging laws that exist to control and guide our relational behaviour, and protect us from ourselves so that we can maximise our opportunities for mutual progress. Any neglect or disregard of these spiritual and moral laws has devastating consequences for us. We are reminded of this every day in our newspapers and on television, and also in our daily interaction with people, whether at work or at home. If we take the time to honestly observe human behaviour in action around our world, we have no option but to conclude that in general, we have not understood nor mastered the spiritual and moral laws that bring out the best in people. All too often we have become masters at bringing out the worst in ourselves and others.

Bringing it all together

Entrepreneurial, Spiritual, and *Moral* laws provide a distinct and vital connection between the purpose, goals and the results that are achieved in a business (see Figure 6). This will become more apparent through the remainder of the book as we explore these laws and their application to how we function as individuals and teams in a business.

By understanding not only the laws themselves, which some readers might already be familiar with, but also how they interconnect and apply to our work, we will better understand how any person's career and any business can reach its full potential.

Figure 6

The Elite Mission

The deepest part of the human spirit is stirred by the merged fear, excitement and purpose of achieving an elite goal

Elite teams in any sphere of life whether sport, military, medical or business, are defined by the standards that determine entry to them. Elite standards create elite performance when they become second nature to the people that are trained by them. It is the standards themselves that form the benchmark to which people must aspire and work towards if they are to be selected for an elite team and be fit for the task.

There is never a shortage of people who are prepared to work incredibly hard to meet the high standards imposed by an inspired goal. We find these people in dance studios, sports clubs, military academies, recording studios, school class rooms, businesses and restaurant kitchens. They can be found in every walk of life. People just like everyone else except for one huge difference. They know what they love to do. They have discovered and defined their unique gift, and their desire to express it motivates them to do what it takes to achieve their goals.

People are not elite performers *because* they work on honing their skills; they work on honing their skills *because* as highly motivated individuals they seek opportunities that demand more skill, more challenge, more risk and bigger rewards – opportunities that match their ambition. Their 'let me show you what I can do' attitude is what sets them apart. Although the number of people who readily display this attitude and work ethic might at first glance, seem to be relatively small, the number of 'hidden' potential elite performers in organisations is significant. They exist at all levels. But, where corporate culture does not specifically encourage entrepreneurial expression, they are usually too unsure of themselves to display their potential.

People who seek to be part of an elite team have a radically different perspective of what is possible. They are not constrained by the question *"What needs be achieved"*, but in asking a different question, *"What can we achieve?"* they are liberated at work.

The Elite Mission

An elite mission is a response to an elite goal. An ordinary goal does not inspire or require an elite mission; and where only ordinary results are expected, only ordinary results are produced.

An elite goal, when we first hear about it, is usually rejected at first by our minds – it's just too close to impossible and way outside current experience to be easily embraced. However, when the deepest part of our human spirit gets stirred by the merged fear, excitement, pleasure and purpose of an elite goal, we get drawn towards its possibility. There is hardly a human heart that will not respond to the invitation to be part of a team pursuing an elite opportunity for a noble cause, where each member's unique value will be decisive in determining its success and where each person shares in its achievement and reward. We were created this way and will almost always respond to a leader who has the courage to break the mould and take the risk of setting an elite goal.

An elite mission will be the ultimate test of a person's highest skill, relationships, commitment and dogged perseverance. It is defined by a purpose that unifies the team and keeps them motivated and focused even under the greatest difficulties.

Purpose is Everything

What kind of purpose can elicit this kind of response? Only the noblest purposes that will jointly serve our customers', business's and employees' highest interests can attract this kind of response. Business leaders, employees and customers must be able to identify with the purpose individually and collectively; individually, because purpose is the greatest motivator to individual action, and collectively, through confidence that everyone is focused on its fulfilment. Profitability is of course central because it measures the effectiveness of the mission, but it is not its purpose.

Noble purpose goes beyond ordinary purpose. It introduces a new dimension that expands the value a business seeks to provide its customers and investors, and the opportunities available to employees to grow their careers. For example, a company whose purpose was to "advance medical technology" now has the purpose "to lead the world in new patient recovery technologies". Based on this patient and innovation focused purpose, everyone in the company has a new opportunity to respond to the bigger challenge. The company whose purpose it was to "generate electric power" resets its purpose to "the most affordable power in the nation" and the company whose purpose it was to "sell tyres and shock absorbers" resets its purpose to "keeping Britain safe on the road".

In each case the purpose has shifted from the company to its customers. The bar has been raised, and an opportunity has been created to take the business to a new level that requires more value from the organisation; value that requires the full engagement of every employee and a redefining of their contribution.

*

Elite missions are driven by elite goals and high stakes. Leaders of elite missions look to 'ordinary' people to seek out the 'extraordinary' in them. This is based on the belief that extraordinary exists, and is achievable by anyone willing to rise to the challenge. Elite missions always carry with them the small possibility of failure... but not the fear of failure, because 'belief in the mission' is its primary driver. Belief, the kind I am talking about, is only possible if it is personal. A good salary and career prospects are not enough to produce the kind of belief I am referring to.

People need a bigger purpose to live for. People want to be part of something special that they can give their 'heart' to, not just their skill. They want to believe in something that characterises them.

Tristan Hunkin, Group Head of News at UKRD, talks about the elite standard expected and encouraged in the company. *"It is not an easy company to work for – in fact it is probably one of the hardest and most challenging environments I have worked in during my twenty year career. We have robust conversations – courageous conversations – that could be avoided at any other company, or chucked over to HR to sort out. But at UKRD we aren't just authorised to have those conversations – we are expected to have them – because otherwise we aren't living the values ourselves.*

"And that happens at all levels in the organisation. All members of staff have the chief executive's mobile number in case they need to speak directly to or challenge him.

"Our people are put at the centre of the decisions we take – or are given the authority to take them themselves in order to accelerate their own development."

The Corporate Mission

An elite vision *for* a company must have an elite mission *to* customers. This mission must be communicated and understood throughout an organisation; calling for and relying on every person's highest engagement in executing the strategic plan. This is the decisive force that will set the company apart from competitors, giving it an unassailable and sustained competitive advantage. It will also create the platform to achieve its highest profit potential, but only if the corporate mission is translated into smaller elite team missions where every team shapes their decisive role and every team member plays their decisive and unique part. Only then will *personal impact* become a reality.

The Team Mission

An elite team mission, shaped and honed by its leader, will be inspired by the company's vision and mission, and will harness the unique contributions of each individual in the team for a 'cause' that is distinctly personal and highly motivating that will strategically impact customers and the company. It will be much bigger than any individual could accomplish on their own including the leader, and bigger than the team itself, thereby demanding significant commitment and synergy between each person to accomplish it. It is through this commitment and synergy that each team member gets to experience what it is like to be part of a committed group of individuals who are changing the future of their customers, their organisation and through this, their own futures.

The Individual Mission

The elite standard of the corporate and team mission is not an impediment to success but the reason for success. It helps individuals find such meaning and purpose in their work that they become fully motivated to develop and maximise their contribution. This defines a person's individual mission. As they are brought face to face with the challenges and rewards of what they have taken on, they rise to the challenge; changing their thinking, habits, performance and future.

*

Elite missions usually succeed for three reasons. These factors, now revisited, demonstrate quite clearly why so many 'ordinary' missions without an elite challenge to participants often deliver disappointing results. They also demonstrate what sets winning companies apart from losing companies.

Entrepreneurial drive

Entrepreneurial drive creates the capacity within people to achieve big goals. It is not a drive for money but a drive to achieve. This drive is the catalyst that produces the necessary commitment and resourcefulness in people to achieve goals significantly beyond their current experience. Entrepreneurial drive is what enables people to see beyond the obstacles that will always threaten to derail an elite mission, and to dig deep to find internal resources they have never tapped into, but must do, if they are to succeed. They know that financial reward follows successful execution.

Consequence

Consequence connects people to results through shared risk and reward at a personal level. There must be potential for gain and loss at a personal level as a result of decisions, actions and results. This is not just about money and may not be about money at all for some, but it is always about what we care deeply about – what is really at stake for us personally if we succeed or fail in our mission. Without consequence there is no commitment, without commitment there is no competitive engagement and without competitive engagement there can be no elite mission. The greater the consequences for us in the decisions and actions we take, the greater the quality of those decisions and actions.

Competitive Engagement

Competitive engagement is about the intensity of desire to succeed, and the focus applied to a personal, team and corporate mission. It draws on the power of entrepreneurial drive and the reality of consequence in a display of intense human effort to achieve a mission that is cared about deeply.

The Corporate Imperative

There is no middle ground for companies who want the best from themselves and for themselves. It is not about trying harder at things attempted before, but about crossing the great divide into a new paradigm of thinking and performance. Crossing the divide requires belief that an elite mission is achievable, and courage to halt any disconnection between the company and its employees that dilutes and weakens the corporate vision and strategy.

Questions to consider

• Does your company distinguish between an 'outward looking' purpose defined by customer needs and an 'inward looking' goal to maximise profit?

• Does your company have a value system and culture that recognises moral, spiritual and entrepreneurial integrity?

• Are you a leader who raises the bar of what is possible by inspiring employees to take on elite business missions?

Part 3

Unique Ability

Defining Unique Ability

Ability that sets every person apart from every other person in every business on the planet

Potential to produce high impact value in the workplace that is unique to you is one of your most valuable gifts. It is what sets you apart from every other person in every business on the planet. Your unique ability contains the DNA from which your unique *personal impact* is derived and is the gateway through which your best opportunities and greatest rewards lie when it is defined and developed. It is also what your team, company and customers will become dependent on you for, making you indispensable and economically secure.

Unique ability is the ability a person has to do things in a unique way or have a unique perspective that enables them to see solutions to problems that others do not see. This ability can be clearly recognised by others when displayed, and is the result of the *unique talent* that resides deep within every person, that is often not recognised by them. When it is recognised by a person, brought to the fore and developed, coupled to their skill set and then ignited by their entrepreneurial drive, the resulting boost in ability and confidence produces *personal impact* that is entirely unique to them.

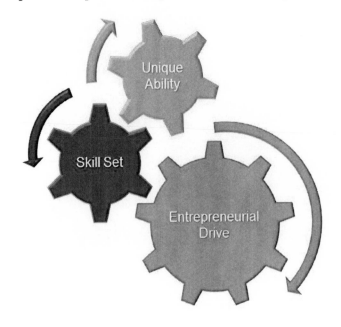

Figure 7

Components of Unique Ability

Our ability to recognise, define and apply our own unique ability lies in the knowledge we have of ourselves which ironically, often requires the help of people close to us, to help us see. With reference to figure 8 below, we will now explore the components of unique ability in more detail.

My experience in working with teams in organisations has led me to conclude that the most difficult aspect of this subject is the ability of a person to recognise their own unique talent. However, with the help of colleagues and a little introspective searching, it is usually identified. Many of us have more than one talent and many people seem to be blessed with an abundance of talent. However, it is our unique talent – that single gift that lies deep within us that is often dormant – that will set us apart from everyone else in the workplace, which we must recognise and develop.

Figure 8

Our unique talent is integral to who we are as a person and is always expressed through our personality and character. Our aim is to use our personality to give it flair and our character to give it depth. Our personality is defined by the traits we are born with that make us different while our character is defined by our learned behaviour (good and bad). It is derived from the attitudes and values we have taken on board during our lifetime. Our unique talent once identified and developed, changes the way we view ourselves and how others view us. For example, Mary who is a mortgage advisor in a bank has a unique talent for putting prospective clients at ease. Although a quiet person by nature (personality), her deep appreciation for people and their needs (character) enables her to match the bank's products to her clients' financial needs in a way that makes her bank stand out against its competitors in the minds of her clients (Mary's unique ability). Mary's *personal impact* for the bank is measured by her unmatched sales record.

Our skill set, which provides us with our basic commercial relevance, now takes on new meaning and value in the workplace as the platform from which our unique ability is delivered (see figure 8). Our knowledge, experience and skill that we have thus far accumulated, and that we might not have considered special, now carry new weight and importance. For example, Mary has other colleagues with similar banking knowledge, experience and skill, all essential for the work they do, but it is Mary who stands out from them because she has identified and now applies her unique ability, while her colleagues do not.

Although we might have our unique ability and skill set in place, it is only our entrepreneurial drive (see figure 8) that gives us the confidence and impetus to 'step into' where we have not dared go before. For example, what gives Mary the confidence she needs to step out and apply her unique ability each day, especially when things are difficult, is her underlying entrepreneurial drive that motivates her each day. Mary, who loves what she does, has a vision to head her department and has taken full ownership of the challenge to do so. She does not expect any personal advancement unless she first delivers exceptional value to her customers and bank. This is the entrepreneurial ethos she lives by and wins by.

Identifying Unique Ability

As a first step to recognising our own uniqueness, there are many widely used personality profiling tools that help explain our personality traits. However, this is just the beginning of the discovery process. We need to understand what motivates us and how this, in combination with our unique talent, defines our potential for unique accomplishment in the workplace.

It should come as no surprise that it is our colleagues who we work closest with who are best placed to help us, because they observe not only our performance, but also our true character, and not as we like to be seen or pretend to be. They see the best and the worst in us in the context of the daily demands and challenges faced in the workplace.

Although a person's natural talent is an ability that comes easily to them, their unique talent is a little more subtle and deeper. For example, most leaders have a talent for inspiring those they lead, but their unique talents might vary considerably. One leader might inspire others through their ability to communicate their vision, while another leader inspires by demonstrating how a job should be done. Other leaders might inspire through their ability to speak or write.

A practical and helpful exercise in identifying our unique ability is to ask a select group of close colleagues for feedback on the following questions. Comparing and analysing the answers will give us pointers as to what it might be. We can then begin work on further developing ourselves along the lines we have identified.

1. How would you describe the value I bring to the team and business?

2. What skill makes me stand out as different to others?

3. Do I influence others, and if so, how?

4. What are my best and worst character traits?

5. How would you describe my unique ability? (What I am able to do that no one else can)

6. Can you describe the *personal impact* (if any) that I bring to the team and business?

Establishing Personal Uniqueness

Your Gateway to delivering Personal Impact

In this section we explore the first four *Laws of Noble Enterprise* to achieve four important goals:

1. Preparing for a bigger future.
2. Unlocking unique value.
3. Having a passion to perform.
4. Understanding that our 'personal brand' is our equity.

Preparing for a Bigger Future

Businesses that want a significant lift in performance will need to challenge current standards. But to do this, a strong foundation for real change will, in many cases, first need to be established in the minds and hearts of employees. The first entrepreneurial law *Invite Change* is what is needed to do this. Mary Kay Ash, founder of Mary Kay Cosmetics, Inc. said these now famous words: *"There are three types of people in this world: those who make things happen, those who watch things happen and those who wonder what happened."*

People who make things happen are people who take the initiative in shaping the future that they want. They knowingly embrace change because they are not afraid of it, for they know that within change lies their opportunity. By inviting change they prepare themselves personally to be on the lookout for opportunities that will shape their future. The preparation they undertake is not easy. It always requires an honest response to an honest reality check. People who make things happen understand that economic obsolescence is the main 'enemy' of every business and career – not competitors. They know from experience that obsolescence is an 'enemy' that is always 'defeated' by being fully prepared to continuously redefine relevance to customers and then vigorously following this up by creating new value for them. Inviting change is their first step to having *personal impact* in a business.

People who watch things happen are people who resist change. Fear or pride causes stagnation in their careers and therefore within the businesses in which they work. Through fear or stagnation they exclude themselves from the excitement of new opportunities, not recognising them for what they are. Instead they view them as an increase in workload or as a threat to their job.

People who wonder what happened are usually so disengaged from the reality of the economic world around them, that if they are not already unemployed, they probably will be soon.

Inviting change is the chief weapon we have against personal economic obsolescence irrespective of our work role. It is also the first law that helps us establish our personal uniqueness in the workplace, because we must initiate the important changes within ourselves and our work that will bring out the best in us. Meeting the demands of staying economically relevant in a fast changing global and local business environment goes beyond simply making cosmetic adjustments to the way things are done. What is required is a comprehensive re-look at the values, beliefs and perspectives that drive our thinking and behaviour. This is why when we apply the principle of inviting change to ourselves, we need the support of the moral law *Significance follows Humility* (see figure 9 below), because the real change needed by us to stay economically relevant often requires deep and honest reflection followed by the courage to change.

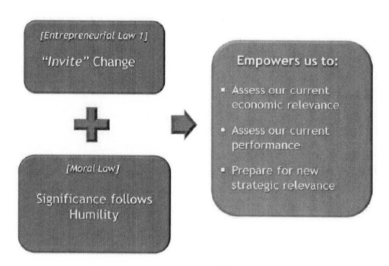

Figure 9
Opportunity demands Continual Change

It is a humbling experience when we realise that the significance we seek in our work lives cannot be 'manufactured' by us or simply claimed by us. It is a virtue other people place on us, which we earn when we demonstrate our value to them by serving them and delivering to them our unique *personal impact*. Our economic value means little until it is actually experienced by customers and colleagues. To experience our value they must be helped by it and the more they are helped, the more significance they place on us.

> *Personal change is our weapon*
> *against economic absolescence*

Humility does not diminish power, intelligence, purpose, opportunity or fulfilment. It is in fact the door to all these things, and to becoming everything we were created to be. The workplace is full of frustrated people who would 'rather be doing something else' but are not sure what this 'something else' is. Is it possible that for many of these people, the problem is not the *type* of work they do, because they started their careers enthusiastically, but that obsolescence is setting in because they are not keeping pace with change? When we realise that our fulfilment and significance comes from how others appreciate what we do for them, we can serve our way to greatness. If we do not purposefully grow our life, it will shrink. Inviting change is about inviting growth; it keeps us adaptable and relevant. It enables us to do things this week that we were unable or afraid to attempt last week. Inviting change is the 'tool' we use to prepare ourselves to confidently launch into new things that inspire the confidence of our customers and colleagues in us. Humility means that we must be honest about the changes we need to make in our own lives. Only we can decide where we need to change and why we need to change.

A few years ago I was invited by the chief executive of Professional Provident Society in South Africa to work with his regional management team. Massive political and social change in the country and a significant increase in competition for an emerging market had left them unprepared for the challenge. My task was to introduce an entrepreneurial culture to help them position and sell their unique financial product range.

Frans Lombard, a senior team member had this to say about his experience and how he was challenged by the entrepreneurial principles that were presented. *"It brought me to a grinding halt, to re-think what and who was really important to ensure the success of my business. It was a journey from the comfort of the restrictive environment where I defended my income with ease, to an entrepreneurial way of life and thinking, where there is significant financial reward for smashing targets, but my fear of beating current performance standards must first be conquered!"*

His colleague Wimpie Mouton shared this insight. *"It made me think and left me nowhere to hide if I was honest with myself."* Someone else said, *"The element of fear has dropped drastically."*

A Bigger Future

Organisations and people that sign up for the journey to a bigger future share five characteristics:

• The unavoidable pain that change requires is no longer avoided. Instead change is embraced as the means to *personal impact* and the high levels of personal fulfilment and reward that accompany it.

• Leaders and staff see opportunity beyond the constant pressure of change. It is what makes their vision real and change meaningful. It is what enables corporate and personal goals to be envisioned and entrenched in the minds and hearts of employees.

• Leaders and staff develop the courage to continually reinvent themselves and their roles to stay at the top of their game. Serving their customer's highest interests is what propels their impact and creates their significance.

• Employees develop an unswerving belief in their ability to ensure their own economic future. It is on this platform of confidence that the business's strategy and objectives are launched and executed.

• The demand to stay 'change fit' that requires personal sacrifice is not an onerous chore but a personal challenge employees embrace as they keep growing and achieving.

Unlocking Unique Value

We establish personal uniqueness in the workplace when we create an air of expectancy among colleagues, bosses and customers about the uniqueness of our work, how we go about it, and its impact on the business. Unique value is what is produced for the business when we apply our unique ability in practical ways, with others, to maximise opportunities and solve real problems.

What Does Unique Value Mean?

For a person's work to qualify as having unique value, it must satisfy two requirements. It must be both valuable to the business and unique to an individual. In other words it is recognisable value that helps advance a business in a unique *way*. It could either be the *nature* of the work itself or the *way* ordinary and often repetitive work is elevated to become special and unique, or a combination of both.

> **What your team needs that it can get only from you**

It means taking our skill set (knowledge, skills and experience) which could be similar to others, and purposefully applying our personality, character, and unique talent to it to transform our work into a unique 'art' form. This takes practice and perseverance but the goal is to develop our own *strategic craft* that will enable us to produce impact on demand that is recognised and valued by our team, our company and our customers. It is this strategic craft that successful entrepreneurs develop, that make their distinctiveness so easily recognisable and valuable. It also empowers them to succeed at whatever they do, often against difficult odds. Employees can do the same wherever they work.

For example, call centre team leader Mary Flanagan's recognisable unique value is how she is able to inspire her team so that service targets are beaten year after year (*nature* of the work). No one has ever been able to achieve what Mary achieves.

The engaging enthusiasm for interacting with customers that lorry driver Bob Spencer displays on his delivery rounds (the *way* repetitive work is elevated), has become his recognisable unique value. Bob's unique talent for appreciating people, combined with his personality and character, have enabled him to be an ambassador for the supermarket he works for.

When Tim Watson, Commercial Manager of Yorkshire Coast Radio, was asked what his customers expect that is unique, this was his reply: *"An unrivalled level of passion, enthusiasm and creativity. They expect to feel we are totally committed to them, their businesses, their lifestyle, their community."*

Unique value can be expressed in a variety of ways in a business including the way we think, speak, write, lead, sell, design, innovate, solve problems, build relationships, apply wisdom and knowledge and anticipate future challenges, or any combination of these aspects of work.

Just producing something unique does not necessarily mean it has any practical commercial use in a team or company. It must solve a problem of some description that our customers or organisation cannot solve themselves, or it must enable them to achieve an important new opportunity we have initiated for them.

A person's unique value qualifies as *personal impact* when it advances a business. Mary Flanagan's call centre for solving customer queries is so successful that it also woos customers to buy more, something no one has accomplished in the company before. She and her team now enjoy an additional financial incentive. Bob Spencer, the friendly face for online grocery deliveries, has the highest reorder rate in the company because he has made buying groceries an experience for his customers. He too earns more than his colleagues. If either Mary or Bob resign, their team, company and customers lose someone whose value cannot be replaced.

Why Belief is Important?

Our unique value is also an expression of what we believe about ourselves and what we believe we are capable of achieving. The greater our belief, the more of our potential is released. The less our belief, the more we hinder our ability to achieve. The importance of this in professional sport and other challenging endeavours is well documented and is now an advanced science. We are not an accident of nature, but a unique masterpiece of creation with a unique gift, personality, purpose and future. Every one of us has immense value to offer but we must first believe this is true of ourselves.

Therefore, if the work performance of employees is limited to the level of belief they have in what they are capable of achieving, then it follows that the financial results they produce is also a reflection of that belief. By growing our belief in our potential to create unique value we are able to push the limits of our impact on customers and our business. This is an important call for leaders – to influence the way people think about themselves, their customers and the people they work with. This is needed to help employees grasp a sense of the greatness that is possible, and to build the entrepreneurial drive necessary to achieve it.

This is why *Create Unique Value*, the second entrepreneurial law (see figure 10 below) is supported by the spiritual law *Our Potential lies in our Belief that it is Unlimited.*

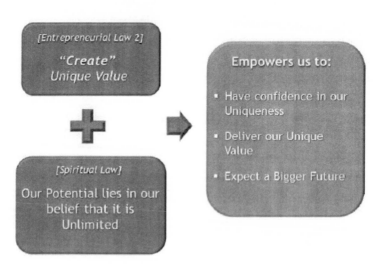

Figure 10

Seeing the Potential in Ourselves Unlocks our Uniqueness

Journey to unlock Unique Value

Individuals who are determined to deliver unique value make it a priority to work hard on:

• Identifying their unique ability.

• Honing their strategic craft.

• Applying their unique value to products and services in their company.

• Creating opportunities to deliver their unique value.

• Developing a reputation for their unique value.

Passion to Perform

Defining our Purpose for work is the third entrepreneurial law. It is the most significant action we can take in our career. Taking time to do this will differentiate us from the majority of people, for whom work has little purpose beyond meeting personal financial needs. Defining purpose in our work will free us from the shackles that make work a burden, and open our thinking to possibilities that will transform our lives.

Defining our *personal work mission* is to define *what* our life's work *is* and *why* it is important to us. This overarching and higher purpose brings the meaning and perspective we need for each work day, and with it, the eagerness to take on the challenges of accomplishing our team and company mission as the means to accomplishing our own personal work mission. For example Peter Haywood, a civil engineer, has made his personal work mission to *'design remarkable bridges'* because he derives fulfilment from the complexity and permanence of his work. As a result, Peter was always first to take on the most challenging assignments for his company. Not surprisingly, he is now their chief designer and head of the department. Susan Cooke, an executive assistant, has made her personal work mission *'chief executive effectiveness'* because she derives enormous satisfaction from managing the multi-faceteddemands made on her boss's time that threaten to erode his effectiveness. She has worked for four of the country's most senior chief executives during a career spanning thirty years.

Being 'mission minded' is to be 'challenge minded' and this makes us dig deep into the resources of our personal uniqueness.

Linking Purpose, Performance and Money

There is a significant difference between the value produced by employees who live by a *personal work mission* and those who do not. This is because there is a causal link between purpose and achievement. In an elite team the sense of purpose that team members experience is expressed in the goals they set. Purpose is the guiding characteristic they all share. It is individual team members' own sense of personal purpose that gives them the desire to achieve and take on the team's business mission. The more difficult the goal is to achieve, the more rewarding it is for them. Elite team members distinguish themselves from dreamers and non-achievers by the challenges they are prepared to take on, because they are motivated by purpose. They have learnt to apply the disciplines of focus and determination in the face of distraction and lesser priorities that rob many others of achieving what they are capable of.

> ## Defining a Personal Work Misssion

Our ability to bring lasting value to the workplace will be as small or as great as the purpose we are serving. The less selfish our intentions, the greater our influence will be, because it is only when we are motivated by a purpose that is beyond ourselves and our own immediate needs, that we are free to perform at our best. How we view ourselves, our work, our colleagues, our company and our customers are all directly affected by our own underlying personal purpose or lack of purpose.

Money is important to all of us and a vital and motivating component of our personal work mission. When we allow our purpose to define what we believe we are worth and not our employer, it will lift the limits of what we earn.

Purpose is Vital

Our work life is tough and getting tougher. It is not for the faint-hearted. It is a marathon race where there are no spectators, only committed competitors or reluctant participants. Committed competitors have a vision and a purpose and use every mile as training for the next. They get stronger the further they go. While they sweat and strain they also enjoy the event and the camaraderie of other competitors. They will 'win' their race – the achievement of their mission.

On the other hand, reluctant participants wonder how they got into the race in the first place, and often look for a way out. "Work has to be better than this," they say. "There must be an easier road," they will argue. They say this this because they do not have a 'race' to win, because they do not have a purpose to fulfil.

We can know how purpose driven our 'race' is by the level of energy, direction, motivation and fulfilment we experience as we face and overcome the daily challenges of our work life.

From Purpose to Cause

The moral law *The greater our Purpose, the greater our Motivation*, that accompanies the third entrepreneurial law (see figure 11 below), encourages us to elevate purpose into a cause. A cause goes beyond pleasing customers and making money. It also has the good of society as its objective, thereby providing an important element of a business's sustainability. So, when we elevate our *personal work mission* to a *cause* we can serve and an opportunity to leave a legacy after we are no longer there, our motivation will have no limits. This will happen in companies that are brave enough to define their corporate missions in terms of a cause, and then challenge employees to do the same with their personal work mission.

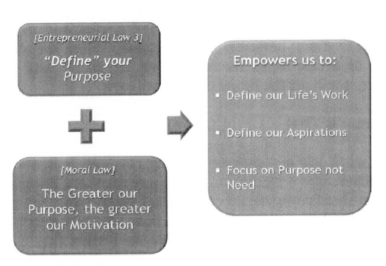

Figure 11

When the Human Spirit Begins to Dance

Employees who have a clearly defined personal work mission will have a noticeably higher level of interest in their work when compared to colleagues who do not. They will:

- Be motivated by purpose rather than need.

- Work towards and achieve their highest aspirations.

- Fully express their talents and uniqueness in their everyday role.

- Be energised by their work.

- No longer work for money only, but to achieve important personal goals.

Your 'Brand' is Your Equity

You have already branded yourself. Everyone you work with, bosses and customers included, perceive your value in a certain way. The question is whether or not it is the brand that you want, and whether it a brand you are proud of. Of even greater importance is whether the people you interact with in the workplace find your brand attractive, sincere and of value. In other words, (as in any product or service) can they trust what they see? Will they 'buy you' without reservation, and will they recommend you to others?

The final step in establishing our personal uniqueness in the workplace is to *Shape our Personal Brand* – the fourth entrepreneurial law. We all have a *personal brand* that contains the perceived economic value our employer, our team and our customers place on us, whether we are aware of it or not. This perceived economic value by others is our 'brand equity'. It determines our earning power in the same way that a company has brand equity in the minds of its customers, thereby determining how much they are prepared to pay for its products or services.

> *Define your Difference,*
> *Maximise your Impact*

Your personal brand is your daily transportable advertisement that reminds your company and customers of what you are capable of achieving for them. It goes everywhere you go and is always sending a message – good or bad. Your current income has been determined by you through your current personal brand. By introducing *personal impact* into your brand, you acquire an exclusive method of lifting the lid on your earning power.

Shaping a Personal Brand

A good brand always requires consistency. As consumers we tend to attach our most recent experience of a product or service to its brand, whether it was a good experience or bad one. Our memories of past good experiences are quickly replaced by our most recent bad experience. I am often amazed at large corporations who spend hundreds of millions on their brand and its awareness, but allow it to be trashed by some front line employee who doesn't care.

How do we best go about building a personal brand that will serve our company's best interests and our own? Just like any other product brand, the success of our personal brand is based on how well we have managed to define our difference and maximise our impact. It comprises our Unique Ability (*unique talent, personality and character*), coupled to our Skill Set (*knowledge, experience and skill*) ignited by our Entrepreneurial Drive (*ownership, passion and vision*).

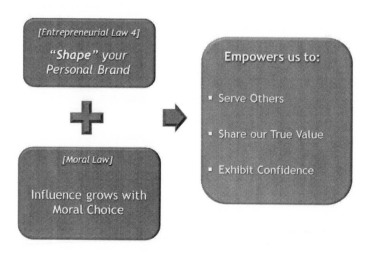

Figure 12
Destiny and Purpose flow from the Moral Choices we make

Because our personality and character are part of our personal brand, and because we need to develop brand consistency, a particularly difficult thing for us humans to achieve, we need to take cognisance of the moral choices we make that form our character. The moral law **Influence grows with Moral Choice** (see figure 12 above) challenges us to do the right thing. A good personal brand can take years to develop and only minutes to destroy. We must take care to remember that our personal brand works for us or against us depending on the most recent experience of our 'customers'. Every spoken word and action counts. It goes without saying then, that we should take great care in building and protecting it.

More than Performance

> *Share your True Value - build*
> *Brand Equity that Lasts*

Since the purpose of our personal brand is to build our 'brand equity' in the eyes of other people, we need to 'package' our value with personal integrity and morality that will make us attractive to our customers. We all need to improve our brands by looking carefully at the values and motives behind our intentions. Our brand works for us not because we constantly promote ourselves (that would undermine our integrity), but because we have learnt to 'live' our value confidently, trusting others to promote us. This enables us to not be distracted from our chosen purpose, believing that our true self will always be our best self.

Building a strong personal brand means:

• Being recognised for a unique contribution to the business.

• Customers and your organisation have ongoing expectations of new value from you.

• Customers (internal and external) promote your value to others without you knowing.

• Being sure of what customers really think of your contribution to them.

• Your name is considered when new opportunities are being planned.

Questions to consider

• Are employees in your company recognised for their potential unique ability and entrepreneurial drive, or are work roles predetermined and limited by currently perceived company needs?

• Are employees considered part of your company's brand equity?

Part 4

Entrepreneurial Drive

The Entrepreneurial Mind-Set

The only mind-set that has ever been able to maximise value for customers and profits for a business on a sustainable basis

Entrepreneurial drive in the workplace can be easily identified by observing the actions of people who have an entrepreneurial mind-set. Their distinctiveness is displayed by their motivation and willingness to stretch themselves in delivering the highest value possible to their 'customers' and in impacting the business wherever they are able to do so. People who do not display these characteristics do not have entrepreneurial drive.

To better understand why an entrepreneurial mind-set defies mediocrity and is the driving force behind the commercial success of any business or career, we need to briefly compare it to two other common workplace mind-sets and the results they produce. Most organisations display a combination of these mind-sets in varying degrees.

Entitlement Mind-Set

A person with an 'Entitlement Mind-Set' believes they are entitled to a living that has no relation to any value produced. They lack enthusiasm and avoid any risk whatsoever, looking to their employer or their government as their benefactor. The implications of this total 'economic disconnect' to a business and its customers should normally render this person unemployable, although paradoxically there are still such people earning a wage. They also unknowingly undermine their company's results.

Where does such a mind-set originate from? I believe when the socialistic philosophy that underpins a welfare state goes beyond the noble purpose of protecting only the most vulnerable of people, it will begin to seep into main stream society and eventually into main stream business. When it does, it kills initiative and responsibility and stifles business growth. It is an economic 'illness' that if allowed to spread can even stifle a nation's economy.

Job Mind-Set

The 'Job Mind-Set' describes the majority of employees in the workplace. People with this mind-set view work and their careers primarily as a necessary trade of time and skill for the money they need to make a living or fund a chosen life style. Although this approach to work, found in highly skilled as well as lower skilled people, does provide valuable service to customers and a company, *personal impact* is never a possibility. The person with a 'Job Mind-Set' usually avoids the responsibility and effort required to create the unique difference that will define their impact. They also avoid accepting the consequences for lack of achievement.

The general lack of a higher purpose (other than making a living or funding a certain life style), together with an unwillingness to be stretched uncomfortably to achieve more, makes it highly unlikely that employees in this category will truly identify in any personal way with a company's customers and with its vision and mission.

People with a job mind-set generally see work as a 'right' and not an opportunity that must be earned. They will be inclined to do only what is required of them (even though they do a good job) without ever discovering what they might be capable of. Mediocrity is often their standard although they will seldom realise it.

Entrepreneurial Mind-Set

The highly motivating entrepreneurial mind-set that distinguishes people who consistently create *personal impact* and reach their career and earning potential, from people whose 'job mind-set' severely limits their commercial value and potential, or worse, whose 'entitlement mind-set' denies them economic relevance, is based on the understanding that financial reward and personal opportunity are entirely governed by the degree to which 'customers' and employers value what is done for them. A person with an entrepreneurial mind-set is fuelled by purpose and a passion to achieve goals that are both challenging and highly personal. They also display the resourceful perseverance needed to overcome obstacles in their pursuit of excellence. Anyone can develop an entrepreneurial mind-set if they give themselves a reason to do so and are determined to apply themselves.

Employees who display entrepreneurial drive produce the commercial actions to match. They become so fully engaged in their company's business that they become unstoppable in bringing all their skill, passion and creativity to bear in creating and delivering, through their work, the highest value they can for customers and the business. They get promoted and are continually offered new opportunities. They also have sufficient confidence in their own unique brand of transportable impact, that should they decide to change employer, they are able to do so without difficulty. When this level of commitment and impact occurs in a business there can be only one result... the fulfilment of the highest aspirations for customers, investors and employees.

Anything less than this standard disconnects people from the vision of the business, their sense of purpose, the importance to them of customers and the unique opportunity they could own to grow their personal future within a growing business.

Mission to Impact Customers

An employee with an entrepreneurial mind-set has two categories of customer and a mission to impact both. Their customers are external paying customers *and* the company that employs and pays them. They fully realise that external customers are a business's source of revenue... and *how much* they spend is determined by the *value* delivered to them. Therefore creating high impact value becomes their primary objective. This impact equates to cash when applied to external paying customers and value and efficiency when applied internally to the business. Added together, they form the basis of the business's profitability.

Impact on customers comes in a variety of ways from product innovation to everyday service innovation. The concept applies to every business, every team within a business and every individual in every team.

The key question that should occupy an employee's mind is the degree of influence (positive or negative) they have on value, efficiency and cash flow. Tristan Hunkin of UKRD says of his role: *"I'm given a huge amount of autonomy – but know that with that autonomy comes a huge amount of responsibility, not just to deliver what is expected of me but to look for ways of over-delivering and exceeding the expectations of our clients, listeners and staff."*

> *Employees are never a neutral factor in the minds of customers*

Employees are never a neutral factor in the minds of customers, and therefore never neutral in their influence on customer spend. Employees influence a company's 'brand equity' all the time, enhancing or damaging it in the eyes of customers, thereby increasing or decreasing cash flow. This 'employee brand equity' although sometimes invisible, is always tangible to customers. It is embedded in the design and production processes of products as well as in administrative processes. But it becomes highly visible wherever there is any direct interaction with customers.

Every customer has an expectation of a company based on their past experience with a product or person. When employees demonstrate a 'will to please customers', normal service expectations are met and the company's brand is protected, however when expectations are exceeded because employees demonstrate a 'will to *impact* customers', value is added to a company's brand. However, where interaction is void of any motivation to please, brand value is reduced and so is customer spend.

Only recently I witnessed how a personal banker, following up on my behalf with another department with whom I had made a simple request, faced a 'brick wall' with a staff member for whom this was clearly an irritation in their day. Clearly the front desk was trying to help, but the back room person made no connection between me as a customer and the salary she earned.

An entrepreneurial mind-set is the critical link to keeping a company 'alive' and its employees motivated and empowered to keep raising the standard of the value they create for their customers and the business. When this mind-set is embedded in an organisation the collective desire to perform for customers significantly raises the value being delivered to them. This principle has monumental implications for every company, its customers, its investors, its employees and for society as a whole. It is this principle that is at the heart of every successful enterprise. Where this principle is not found in a business, its results are inevitably diminished.

An entrepreneurial mind-set is a necessity not only for start-up or high growth businesses, but for every business irrespective of its size or maturity. Its presence is vital for keeping a business innovative and at the cutting edge of understanding customer need and delivering the impact necessary to secure their spend. When it is restricted or not actively encouraged and rewarded in an organisation, customer experience will be blunted and what they spend reduced. It will also dull the efficiency of operations within a business. Without it a business is simply unable to do keep pace with the change necessary to keep it relevant and profitable, resulting in decline and eventual failure if things are not corrected.

Therefore, taking a business to the next level is not just about its products and strategy. It is also about every person who works in the business taking their commercial value to the next level. This means going beyond just 'doing a good job', to the level of *creating a unique brand of impact for customers*, whether they are internal or external customers or both.

Entrepreneurial drive is that uniquely human characteristic that every business needs, because it enables the people who work in it to recognise opportunity and then pursue it. It finds expression in many different ways, but it always provides the 'spark' needed to ignite motivation and engagement *and* the power to sustain performance.

Changing Mind-Sets

Whatever our background and the experiences that might have shaped us and our attitudes, ultimately the mind-set we adopt for our future is a choice we make. We have the power to choose what we make of the life we have been given and this means that we have the power to change our mind-set if we want to, and with it our opportunities and future. The question of whether or not an employee can have an entrepreneurial mind-set is a valid one. But when an employee recognises that their career is their 'business', and that the principles for building their earning potential are the same principles used by entrepreneurs in building a business, then an entrepreneurial mind-set becomes essential to them.

The purpose of this book is to present the 'entrepreneurial employee' alternative in a way that will help business owners and chief executives to recognise the value and importance of this for their businesses, and then encourage their employees at all levels to take up the challenge.

Creating New Opportunities

*Growing our opportunities and building our rewards is entirely
determined by how much customers value what we do for them*

In this section we will discover how to apply our entrepreneurial
drive to create new opportunities. We will explore the next three
Laws of Noble Enterprise as an aid to understanding three powerful
concepts:

1. Anything is possible.
2. Taking ownership of new opportunities.
3. The shift from service to impact.

Anything is Possible

Embrace Risk and Reward, the fifth entrepreneurial law, enables us to reach for the goals and rewards we believe strongly enough in and want to achieve, but are fearful of attempting. Embracing risk and reward is that part of the entrepreneurial mind-set that emboldens us to achieve our goals, particularly those that seem impossible to us. Reward follows risk and is not possible without it. Risk is the doorway through which we must all step on a regular basis to create the new opportunities we and our companies need and to receive the new rewards we desire. Our quest for *personal impact* requires that we live by the principle of risk and reward every day. This applies whether are facing the prospect of a new job, tasked with improving a product, developing a new one or leading a team or organisation.

> *Our future is exposed to the*
> *decisions we make today*

The Necessity of Risk & Reward

No great achievement has ever been possible without embracing risk and reward, and no business or career can avoid obsolescence without doing so too. It is essential for every business and every person who works in that business, because risk and reward are the inseparable two sides of the same coin. Viewed with an entrepreneurial mind-set, the prospect of reward generates the desire to achieve something new and more significant. The reality of possible failure is offset by the even greater risk of staying as we are and stagnating. Avoiding risk and reward will cut us off from new opportunities and rewards, thereby ultimately guaranteeing our 'economic stagnation' or worse.

The Power of Risk and Reward

Risk and reward means the potential for gain... and loss, at a personal level. In the workplace this could apply to money, security, opportunity, prestige, fulfilment or a combination of these factors. When we minimise or remove the personal connection to the consequences of our actions, we remove our incentive to perform and our potential to deliver *personal impact*. Risk and reward mean that our reward is conditional on our performance and can be lost, but it also means that when something valuable to us is at risk, we work hard to protect it. This is the entrepreneurial mind-set in action. Risk and reward keep us sharp and personally connected to the goals of our business and the quality of the decisions and actions we take in achieving those goals.

Taking Back Lost Ground

> *Risk and Reward makes our work count at a personal level*

In many work environments there is no formal connection between risk and reward for the majority of employees. There is therefore no real incentive to stretch to achieve more or to protect the company, its customers, its brand and its results. Surrounded by the security and comfort of a largely fixed salary with little to gain or lose, it is easy to see why mediocrity can become the limiting standard. However, when an element of risk and reward is introduced, the limits are removed from what people are prepared to do to achieve what is important. Although this principle already exists to some degree within most companies, it is usually restricted to senior employees and executives but seldom involves an entire organisation.

Risk, Goals & Commitment

The intensity and focus with which a Cup Final sporting event is played is very different from the intensity and focus at a local sports club or school sports meeting. This is because the consequences (stakes) are so different. The higher the stakes are for participants, the greater their competitive commitment.

Small goals carry low risks and low rewards. The bigger our goals the more we have to gain or lose. It is this increased consequence to us that is needed to increase our commitment. It is this consequence (risk and reward at a personal level), that fuels our desire and the level of intensity with which we compete in order to maximise our reward and minimise our loss. This is what is required of us to create *personal impact*.

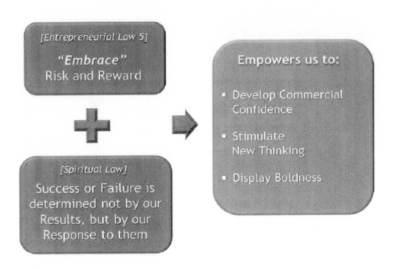

Figure 13
By controlling our Responses to Results we Control our Future

Taking the Sting out of Risk

As humans we have a built-in response mechanism that triggers a combination of mental, emotional and physical responses when we succeed at something or when we fail. In the workplace this can work for us or against us depending on our response. To ensure that all of our workplace successes, failures and mistakes work for us, we must train ourselves to learn from them and 'bank' this new knowledge as valuable experience. The spiritual law, **Success or failure is determined not by our Results, but by our Response to them**, helps us to control our responses appropriately to every result, putting us in control of our future, step by single step. This takes the sting out of risk, and replaces it with the confidence that our growing and learning is preparing us to succeed.

For example, team A plays team B in a hard fought game of football and loses. Team A is very conscious of the mistakes it made on the field and is clearly aware that it did not live up to its training and competitive expectation. It is determined to correct its mistakes before next Saturday's game. Team B, however, were arrogant about their win, claiming that their football prowess won them the game, and that there was nothing to learn from playing team A, a weaker team. Although team A lost and team B won on this occasion, team A banked valuable lessons that will result in future successes, while team B wasted a victory.

Employees and teams who are encouraged by their companies to embrace risk and reward:

• Are motivated by the potential rewards of success.

• Understand the potential risk of failure.

• Become comfortable with the concept of personal risk.

• Are more accountable for the results they produce.

• Limit failure because success is their top priority.

Taking Ownership of New Opportunities

Opportunities for growth and advancement for employees are inseparable from the opportunities they create for their company's growth and advancement. But creating these opportunities requires taking ownership of them, because this is what connects an employee to their team and their team to their company and the company to its customers. Why?

Employees in a business are its sole source for recognising, creating and sustaining opportunity. And the opportunities that must be created every day to avoid obsolescence do not just 'happen', they must be created and vigorously pursued – by everyone! This takes 'ownership' motivated by entrepreneurial drive. When employees are not motivated by entrepreneurial drive, and do not take 'ownership', the very opportunities that produce the income the company relies on for its survival and growth are slowly and unknowingly undermined.

Company leaders who embrace entrepreneurial drive as being vital to employee performance, link opportunities for personal growth for employees, to the opportunities they create for company growth. They understand that opportunities that are not 'owned' and sustained by employees will, over time, disappear. Employees who understand this continually work at the opportunities that keep them employable and advancing in their careers.

Strategic Reality

Every business must realise that their economic survival and growth is dependent on their employees also realising that their own economic survival and growth requires that they adopt two habits. Firstly, an on-going willingness to take collective ownership of customers' needs, and secondly, from an understanding of these needs, to generate new ideas and solutions that can be used to create bigger opportunities for customers, their company and themselves. A person creates new opportunities when they constantly hunt for ways to contribute tangible value that is unique to them, that would otherwise be lost without their personal motivation and attention to making a difference. They own these opportunities when they take personal responsibility to ensure their contribution is delivered in a way that produces its full value. This way of thinking and acting requires more than monetary reward to drive it and sustain it – it requires a shared vision of a company's future.

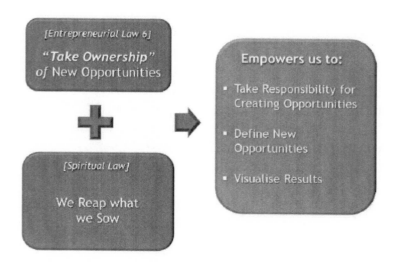

Figure 14
We are only as motivated as our Future Vision is Inspirational

The entrepreneurial law *Take Ownership of New Opportunities* reminds us that our opportunities are entirely our responsibility. We must firstly act to create them, and then secondly, make them personal by persevering to ensure that they are delivered and appreciated. This becomes habitual for people whose entrepreneurial drive makes this principle applicable to every aspect of their work each day.

For example, Tristan Hunkin reflected on his work and the opportunities he must create for his company: *"It is a job I can't see myself outgrowing – because as I change, so does it. I have been lucky enough to write my own job description, ensuring that it stretches and challenges me, while still delivering what is needed by the company."*

Opportunities

Imagine if only one new opportunity to make a difference, even a very small one, was recognised *and* acted upon each day by each employee in a business. That is 21 occasions a month, about 235 a year – per person. If we tried to attach a monetary value to these new opportunities to improve customer service, sales or business efficiencies that might otherwise have been lost, we would be astounded.

Companies miss so many opportunities because so few people are tuned into seeing them, because they have never been expected to think this way. People with an entrepreneurial mind-set thrive in a culture that values fresh thinking, constantly challenges accepted standards of performance and openly recognises and rewards new value.

Owning new opportunities is what grows a business and is central to driving every part of its strategy. Without it, no part of a plan can work to its fullest potential. A company does not own a single opportunity *except* that which is owned in the minds and hearts of employees who vigorously pursue them. Three important questions every leader should be asking are:

1) How 'opportunity minded' is my organisation or team?
2) Do they see the opportunities I see?
3) What could lost opportunities be costing?

Sowing and Reaping

The spiritual law **We Reap what we Sow** (see figure 14) brings into sharp focus that it is our own choices that determine not only our capacity to create opportunity, but whether or not we position ourselves to even see opportunity.

We must realise that there is always a consequence. Everything we are, good and bad, is the direct result of our past decisions and actions. You and I have reaped everything that we have 'sown'. This has directly affected every aspect of our lives including our relationships, opportunities and the assets we own today. We are fully responsible for who we are, what we have done and what we will be in the future. This is both frightening and liberating at the same time. Although we have been the engineers of our current life (a scary thought sometimes), we are also the engineers of the changes we can make and the growth we can pursue to reach our unique potential.

"What do I want my future to look like? What do I need to change?" These are probably the most significant questions we can ask of ourselves. Let's just make sure we *do* ask them. Remember, what we don't sow today, we won't reap tomorrow. As an example, let's see how this spiritual law affects our everyday business lives. Lost a sale lately? Are customers coming back for more? You are reaping what you sowed.

Had problems with members in your team? As a leader you are reaping either what you have sown or what team members have sown. Either way, the reality of what we reap is the reality of what was sown.

Posted disappointing results to shareholders? We must look at what was sown as an entire organisation (perhaps for a lengthy period) to understand what was reaped.

Taking ownership of new opportunities changes our future and this is great news for those of us who are still in the 'race' to achieve something significant. Our future is still in the making and because it is being shaped by us... *only by carefully considering every action today can we control the shape of our reality tomorrow.*

Leaders who want to generate more opportunities must demonstrate to their teams that:

• Change always presents more opportunities than threats.

• Who people are today and what they will become in the future has been, and will be, shaped entirely by their personal choices.

• People are totally responsible and accountable for their own future growth and prospects.

• There are more opportunities today than there have ever been.

• Success is based on the identification and pursuit of meeting the needs of others.

The Shift from Service to Impact

The shift from service to impact is much more than just a major shift in performance. It is also a major shift in the motivation behind a person's actions brought on by an entrepreneurial mind-set. Employees who do not have an entrepreneurial mind-set will always need to be *taught* the basic principles of service, even the need for it, because it does not come naturally to them. In addition, this 'taught attitude' is very difficult to sustain because it is rarely motivated by genuine care for customers. When next you go shopping, take the time to observe how often anyone serving you makes a genuine heart-felt effort to help you, and how often you are made to feel special or important.

However, employees who have an entrepreneurial mind-set have a natural desire to impact their customers because the reality of risk and reward and of ownership and opportunity that they live with and accept as normal, strip away all pretence to genuine customer care. They also understand that service is not a differentiator... impact is, that for most employees service is a text book concept... but impact comes from the heart, service helps customers... but impact changes their spending habits and through that, their economic future.

The sixth Entrepreneurial Law, ***Bond with Customers***, is the key. Empowered by the moral law, ***The less we focus on 'Self' the more our Opportunities Grow***, we soon learn the incredible value of genuinely seeking our customers' best interest before our own. This does not mean that we ignore our own interests but that we strategically link them to the personalised solutions we are seeking to create for our customers. By applying this entrepreneurial and moral law (see figure 15), we give our customers a compelling reason to 'connect' with us on a level that they may not allow with others. Executed properly, this can give us exclusive access and opportunity to meet their most important needs, thereby opening the door into a treasure trove of high value sustainable opportunity.

This combination of entrepreneurial and moral law is so important to us because opportunities to impact customers (always our mission), can so easily become obscured when we put our primary focus on our own reward and not the needs of our customers. Most of us find it difficult not to allow what is so important to us becoming our primary focus, but we must not let that happen if we are to maximise the opportunities we work so hard to create.

Employees become enthused when they see how their unique contributions actually affect customer decisions, and how these customer decisions can in turn affect them, whether in recognition, income, career growth opportunities, work fulfilment or all four. When we know that our customers are *relying* on *us* to provide what they regard as important then the confidence we have in *our own* economic future soars. Bonding with customers is always personal for everyone involved.

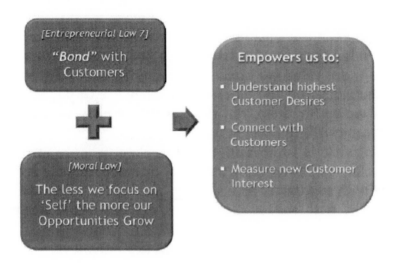

Figure 15
Dependent customers provide Sustainable Opportunity

Customers' Dreams

> *Opportunity lies in our capacity*
> *to focus on the needs of others*

Our biggest opportunities lie beyond our own interests, and are sometimes even hidden in the yet unidentified needs of our customers. Our goal must be to find them. We do this by taking the trouble to gain their trust and understand what is really important to them that they don't usually verbalise to others. This is the secret, and it applies to all our customers, including the boss we report to and the internal team that relies on the work we do. The bond is formed between our customer and us when the customer realises that the value they receive from us is not available from anyone else. The more value we create for them, the more dependent on us they become, and the more willing they are to pay a premium for what we do for them. But this advantageous position requires us to become willing 'servants' to our customers. When we do this and learn what is important to them, they become attracted to the help they get. Eventually a mutual interdependence is formed. Bonding with customers provides the 'glue' of the relationship, and cemented by past impact experiences, enables future needs to be communicated.

Apple is a good example. The company listens very closely to what customers are saying and to what they are likely to want as they create and refine new technologies. The result is that customers will queue all night outside stores to buy the latest model. They also pay a premium to enjoy its new features.

Jaguar is another example, making them fairly immune to recessionary pressures because they meet the stringent standards demanded by customers in the luxury car market. Customers 'bond' with Jaguar because of the differentiated motoring experience they enjoy.

When we bond with our customers it changes the way we view them and the way they view us. We see customers as an opportunity to pursue what we might not have dared consider before. They view us with heightened expectation of fresh value or new strategic help.

This principle can be applied to any employee, team or company that wants to stay ahead of its competition.

Here is a brief check list to help assess whether or not we are bonding with our customers or not; either as an individual, team or company.

• Would my customers experience a setback without me?

• Are my customers aware of my potential?

• Do I constantly re-align myselfto my customers' changing needs?

• Am I close enough to my customers that they share their most important needs?

• Do I surprise my customers with fresh value and impact?

Focus & Discipline

Build an Intense Desire to Succeed

In our journey towards *personal impact* we now explore the next three *Laws of Noble Enterprise,* which will help us achieve the focus and discipline necessary to:

1. Be fully engaged.
2. Be free to focus on impact.
3. Demonstrate personal leadership.

Fully Engaged

The most focused and disciplined people are those who have not only found a purpose that they are enthusiastic about, but have also developed the mental and emotional tools necessary to persevere in their pursuits. All of us can relate to projects that we have started but not completed because we have lost interest in them or simply run out of steam. At a personal level these projects may include getting fit, losing weight or doing a study course. In a business context they may include campaigns to motivate staff, gain new customers or drive new efficiencies. Why, then, do well-meaning efforts to achieve something worthwhile so often dwindle and die? The answer might be twofold. Firstly, the absence of goals that *really* engage us with our purpose, and secondly, the absence of *defined actions* needed to achieve them.

I believe the majority of employee actions are only vaguely directed by goals, if at all. Therefore much of their time and effort is void of the vital ingredients of *what* and *why*, that are so necessary in defining our *personal impact* and engaging us in delivering it. The eighth Entrepreneurial Law, **Set Goals**, ensures that we are clear in our own minds about what it is we want to achieve and why. In a business context, this includes the tangible impact we expect our goals to have on our business. The spiritual law, **Action unlocks Power to Achieve** (see figure 16), comes into play to unleash the motivation and energy within us to achieve our goals – as we begin to *take action*. Taking the specific actions required of our goals is just as important as the goals. It is this focus on our goals, together with the power of our actions, that transforms the use of our time in a way that is not possible without specific goals. But it is vitally important that our goals have personal importance. For it is this ingredient that brings 'life' to our efforts and to the challenge of staying focused and disciplined to see our goals accomplished.

A business goal must have consequence for an individual at a personal level and team level for it to motivate performance. To the degree that it does, it releases not only enthusiasm and purpose, but also a strong and personal desire to succeed, thereby potentially becoming the most potent force within an enterprise. Business goals that employees and teams identify with and embrace, because they have personal significance to them, elevate belief and the desire and the discipline required to achieve them.

The problem that many businesses have is that from an employee point of view, the business goals they are required to pursue are often merely arm's length objectives to be achieved *for* the business. Without goals that employees can identify with at a personal level, there can be no real connection to the objectives of the business. The effect of this on performance should be obvious.

Figure 16
Big goals free the Human Heart and engage the Whole Person

Beyond Financial Goals

Although every company has a documented vision and mission that is customer-centric, when it comes to actually setting *objectives*, these are often mainly financial in nature and beyond the remit of ordinary employees. This has the effect of further distancing them from fully engaging in the business.

It is unusual for a company to give employees a platform to define how they will bring their *personal impact* into play in executing the business plan, and then feed back to them the effect that achieving their goals has had on financial results. More importantly, there should be constant communication between leaders and staff around the strategy for the business, and opportunities for staff to see the gaps to engage entrepreneurially. Leaders of companies desiring to significantly lift performance will make this a priority, giving every team and individual the opportunity to make the achievement of company financial objectives personal.

Goals and Personal Impact

It should now be clear why there is so much more that can be achieved if we allow teams to include their own specific goals on how *they* plan to impact the business to raise the bar of company performance. The self-imposed limits that organisations place on themselves are lifted when its employees set and achieve goals that engage them in delivering the high standard of *personal impact*.

> *Goals give us a wonderful sense of personal freedom and purpose*

In competitive sport, athletes and their teams need to have a belief that is so sure, and a desire to win that is so strong, that victory becomes highly likely if the plan is followed through properly. Sometimes the only thing that sets the winner apart from the loser is their level of belief, desire and commitment to win the prize. It is the same in an elite business team. Belief and desire are captured, clarified, reinforced and sustained when goals are clear and they engage everyone. The more clarity there is to the goal, and the more challenging it is to achieve, the more believable and desirable it becomes.

While the objectives of the business are set by its strategic planners, it is in the detail of how teams and individual members within teams bring their own unique impact in executing the objectives that personalise it for them, thereby defining their *personal impact* on the business. It is the freedom given to people to define their own impact, and then build this into their contribution and link it directly to their earning power and career growth that connects them strategically to the business's mission. Each person should be able to say, *"There is something unique about me and my contribution to implementing the business plan, clarified and documented in my goals, which gives the business its strategic focus and ability to succeed."*

Employees and teams on a mission to create personal impact will:

• Never be fully satisfied with their current level of performance, because there are always new performance boundaries to explore.

• Never be swayed from the focus necessary to achieve important goals.

• Regularly set aside quality time to review mistakes, and learn from them to continually improve performance, while keeping alive an intense desire to succeed.

• Constantly set and review goals, and as a habit, *personalise* them for every team member.

• Keep track of progress towards achieving goals, and when they are achieved or hindered.

Free to Focus on Impact

Adopting the concept of *personal impact* into our daily business practice requires a rethink of how we do many things – including the way we view and value time. While we have no control of how much time we are given, we do have control over how we use it. To *Harness Time*, the ninth entrepreneurial law, we need to view our time at work as our *Gift of Opportunity*, and a personal business asset that must be harnessed and not wasted. When we do, we will also be grateful for it, using it to advance our team's business mission and therefore our own personal work mission.

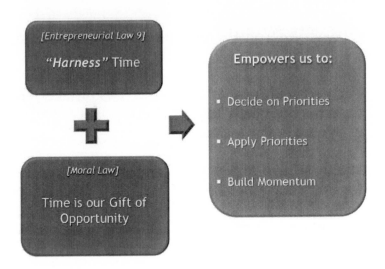

Figure 17
Clearing up the Clutter of Busyness to free up time for Impact

Valuing Time

The majority of employees have the attitude that while they are at work they are in 'company time', hired to achieve company objectives. This outlook precludes them from seeing their time at work as a personal asset and as a result, devalues their appreciation of it. This inevitably diminishes their contribution to their team and company's success, and ultimately their own career prospects.

The well-known concept of Time Management is viewed primarily as a company issue and not a personal one, and when applied to employees, becomes just another company routine to be achieved for the sake of the company. While employees do of course have a sense of the value of time, it is not the same value they would place on it if they were running their own business. But, we *are* using our own time to run our 'own business'. Our career is our business, and what we dream of accomplishing and how we go about it, is entirely up to us. When we see ourselves in 'partnership' with our empoloyer and colleagues in achieving common goals, then our time becomes one of our most valuable assets.

Impact Management

> *Impact Management empowers us to*
> *see time as a friend not an enemy*

The secret to harnessing our time and using it to its full potential is to elevate our thinking about its use by connecting it conceptually to what it is we are trying to achieve. For example, *time management* by definition places emphasis on 'time' and its best use, usually in the context of achieving many things. In this regard, it is often 'how much' we achieve that gives us our sense of achievement, but this does not take into account the 'value' of what is achieved. It may be that some things we have managed to squeeze into our day have little or no effect on the important outcomes of our business.

Impact management, however, makes *personal impact* its primary goal and arranges time accordingly, with a shift in emphasis from 'how much' we achieve to the 'value' of what we achieve. The principle idea here, is that whatever our role in our team, it is our *personal impact* derived from our unique ability that is most needed by it, and therefore this becomes our primary focus. This method of harnessing our time as a personal asset helps us to orchestrate our work life so that we are able to *define, apply* and *achieve* what is most important to us and our team. This does not exclude the ordinary everyday tasks that must be accomplished, as we will soon see. In fact these everyday tasks are now viewed as important things to do in support of, and in preparation for, our *personal impact*. Applying this idea in a team context requires that we also elevate our thinking about how teams work. We will cover this subject in a later chapter.

I can imagine that many readers might be asking themselves, "How do we escape the 'pressure cooker' of overwork and insufficient time that chokes our initiative and prevents us doing the things described in this book?" "How do we find the time to reset our goals and plan to do things differently?" We will now look at a simple technique to achieve this, but it does require some discipline to apply it. To achieve elite goals we must learn to clear up the clutter of busyness that distracts us from developing and delivering our impact.

To help in this process it is useful to consider the demands made on us at work in terms of four well defined segments into which all our activities can fit (see figure 18 below). This can be applied to our individual role, our team, or entire organisation. The four segments are defined by *impact* or *non-impact*, and *focus* or *non-focus* activities. Impact management creates a logical framework whereby employees can create and manage their value, which will enable any enterprise to achieve its full potential. Impact management enables current strategic goals to be achieved, all the daily tasks that keep it functioning to be accomplished, *and* the innovation that will keep it in business tomorrow.

IMPACT MANAGEMENT

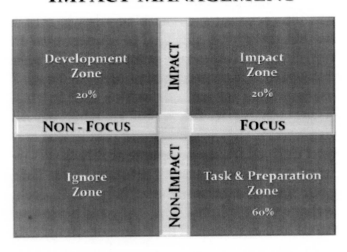

Figure 18

It does this by helping employees to:

1. Redefine their work value.
2. Delegate or ignore what is unimportant.
3. Focus on delivering impact.

Impact Zone

This segment is aimed at helping us maximise our effectiveness by making our impact priorities the centre of our work. This must not be compromised by allowing less important demands to distract us and rob us of our key opportunity. The Impact Zone covers any activity that we have defined as having impact and that is a current focus for us and our team. Although this may occupy perhaps only twenty percent of our available time (or less), it counts for probably eighty percent of our value. This is why it is so important. For a sales person it will be those face to face focused minutes with customers. For a CEO it may be the inspiration they pass on to staff during their direct contact time with them. For a person serving coffee at a Starbucks outlet, it may be their genuine smile and greeting that leaves every customer feeling special. For administrative employees it may be the speed, accuracy and efficiency of their work and ability to anticipate, identify and solve problems.

Task and Preparation Zone

This segment enables us to approach the daily tasks in our work with new appreciation. Although these tasks are non-impact and may often be repetitive, utilising the bulk of our available time, they are still part of our focus because they play an important part in producing our unique value. By approaching these tasks as either preparation for our Impact Zone, or creating extra time for our Impact Zone through our efficiency, we bring new life and creativity to what might have been mundane work. For example, the sales person gets the reporting and paperwork done accurately and quickly to make room for planning a fresh approach and a new presentation to sales prospects. The CEO utilizes his executive assistant to master more of his daily tasks (her Impact Zone) while he focuses on growth strategies for the company. The Starbucks service manager arranges to have a colleague take care of production so she can give customers more of her 'extra touch'. The administrative team get so good at processing and reporting, that they arrange their first ever innovation conference.

The Development Zone

This segment describes the time we set aside to invest in the development of our future impact. It is our personal innovation segment, where we consider new opportunities and challenges that are on the horizon, but not yet imminent and therefore non-focus. This segment is vitally important because it is where we keep ourselves economically fresh and relevant. Ideas that are generated and worked on in the Development Zone today are the source of our Impact Zone tomorrow. Both should enjoy equal importance in our thinking and planning. For example, the sales person researches new sales presentation techniques and how to apply them to current products. The CEO reads new literature on organisational effectiveness and considers how to adopt the principles to his business. The Starbucks service manager has been working on ideas to share with her boss on how to improve sales. The administrative team have identified and been trained on new software that improves the integration of their work with other departments.

The Ignore Zone

The Ignore Zone defines any activity that is non-focus and non-impact. These are typically tasks that come our way that can either be completely ignored, or delegated to someone whose impact is defined by doing them in their support for us. For example, the sales person ignores the temptation to take long lunches. The CEO ignores most of the news journals that are sent to him apart from three carefully selected magazines. The Starbucks service manager ignores the temptation to still get involved with production – something she is so proficient in. The administrative team have identified two reports they produce that are never read and are a complete waste of their time.

Personal Leadership

Delivering *personal impact* requires emotional resilience and a solid platform of motivational beliefs to overcome the many obstacles that must be faced while doing so. Of all the characteristics of our humanity, there is nothing more powerful than our ability to *believe*. Belief is that unshakeable internal spiritual confidence that we can achieve what we have set out to do. It removes the mental boundaries we have erected that limit what we thought possible, and engages us to act in ways that surprise us. Doubt however, does the exact opposite. It kills our dreams, our desires and our will to achieve. It makes us shrink back from challenge and avoid difficulty. It makes us a coward. Doubt therefore, must be faced and dealt with.

Building a belief system to support our goals takes a lot of thinking and personal review, but it is necessary and so worthwhile. Any negative beliefs we have must be replaced by positive ones. This is how we do it.

Believe in Yourself

We all have a choice to make regarding our approach to the future. We can either allow it to overwhelm us and dictate our circumstances, or we can embrace the opportunities it offers, thereby putting us in control of our future. Although the future holds many unknowns, each of us does have what it takes to meet its challenges, even if it means having to dig deep to access our personal reserves of confidence and will power. We must all make the firm decision to *believe* that we are capable of achieving much more than we imagine. This is a prerequisite to achieving more, distinguishing people who are shaping their own future from those who are having it shaped by others.

Believe in your Purpose

Personal confidence in our capability is followed by the desire to connect this to achieving a meaningful purpose. Sustained *belief in our purpose* must be real, coming from deep within us. It can never be contrived and must be real enough to survive all kinds of setbacks both business and personal without being diminished.

The test of whether we truly believe in our purpose or not, is whether the flame of enthusiasm we have for it is kept alive despite our setbacks. People who display entrepreneurial drive are purpose driven and enthusiastic about both their purpose *for* working and their specific purpose *at* work.

Believe in your Value

To ensure that the confidence our company and customers have in us continues to grow, we must keep shaping our unique value in the workplace, and apply it to the changing needs of our company and customers. To do this we must add to the belief we have in ourselves and our purpose, an unwavering *belief in our value*. Each of these elements is an important building block in our personal belief system.

Believe in your Opportunity

Being sure of our value means we become certain of our opportunity and the results it will deliver for our customers and us. This *belief in our opportunity* is the entrepreneurial confidence that comes from truly knowing our customers' needs, and that what we do for them is important to them. It also means being vigilant about meeting the smallest changes to their needs and therefore, in our value to them.

Believe in Your Future

We have built a solid belief system for what we are capable of, our purpose for work, the value we produce and the opportunities we create. We can now also face our economic future with confidence no matter how our circumstances may change. This is the ongoing challenge that people with entrepreneurial drive thrive on, and with confidence. It keeps them learning, relevant, needed and successful.

> *Is our flame of enthusiasm for our purpose still alive despite our setbacks?*

But delivering *personal impact* also requires personal discipline. This does not take brains, it takes 'heart' – the inner strength to keep going when others stop. Discipline is doing what we sometimes do not enjoy, in order to accomplish what is important. It means persevering 'against the odds' to enlarge our vision and capability so that we can take on new challenges and achieve bigger goals. Discipline requires that we develop the right habits for achieving the level of success we expect of ourselves. In so doing, we get stronger and better at our work so that what might have seemed difficult to do six months ago now comes with ease. Discipline keeps this growing process alive.

People with entrepreneurial drive are ordinary people who have learnt to do this. They defeat doubt and fear with an internal belief system that is their armoury against failure, and through personal discipline, they stay on top of their game by seeing themselves as their greatest competitor. No aspect of their thinking or work performance is off limits. They are true professionals who keeping pushing the boundaries of their own performance.

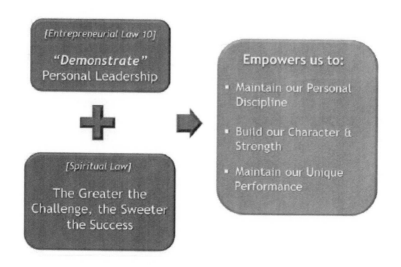

Figure 19
The Greatest Achievers in history have not been the most Gifted, but those who had reason enough not to Give Up

Because tomorrow will be more challenging than today in virtually every respect, we need to embrace the strengthening and growth opportunities that surround us every day, that can better equip us for the futures we are creating. The tenth entrepreneurial law, **Demonstrate Personal Leadership** (see figure 19), reminds us about the discipline and motivation we need to sustain our best levels of performance, and be counted on to deliver our unique ability and impact when necessary. Although this is not always easy to do when conditions get difficult, the spiritual law *The Greater the Challenge, the Sweeter the Success* not only promises us success if we overcome our challenges, but entices us to even greater heights so that we can enjoy even greater success.

Taking up the Challenge

Having created a good enough reason to take up your challenge, here are some strategies to ensure success.

1. Overcome any personal inertia that prevents you from starting out by *"Just Doing It"* as Nike says. It works every time.

2. Once you are working on your project, make discipline a *personal* challenge rather than a necessity required by the project.

3. When endurance is required, create a mind-game where you are in a 'race' that you must win.

4. Be consciously aware of your progress.

Questions to consider

• Considering the three different mind-sets found in businesses, what is the dominant work mind-set in your organisation?

• What does the term 'opportunity' mean for employees in your company?

• To what extent is employee performance linked to financial reward and do they embrace it with enthusiasm?

• Do employees' goals connect them personally to company goals?

Part 5

Unique Teamwork

Understanding Unique Teamwork

Unique Teamwork is a concept that redefines what people are able to achieve as a team, because it enables much higher goals to be visualised and accomplished. Higher goals become possible because they are based on the unique ability that each team member brings to the team. By leveraging this unique ability, a new collective capability is created and a new collective result becomes possible. Unique teamwork is a concept that is already understood and in wide use by the best of the best in sport, entertainment, music, science, the military and many other endeavours. Unique teamwork does two things. It provides a platform for the display of *individual genius* and *team genius*. It provides the sparkle that awes sporting and entertainment audiences, the amazement of space travel and the brilliance of the strategies and precision actions of special-forces military teams.

Ironically, in the field of business the use of this remarkable and powerful idea is rare. The chief reason for this (already covered in detail in parts 1 to 4 of this book), is that the general standard of performance expected of the majority of employees does not extend to them using their unique ability. Unique teamwork is therefore precluded from organisational performance. More often than not, work roles and Key Performance Indicators are prescribed by someone who is not required to perform the role. Because of this, they will have little or no vision of its greater potential, as this is something that can only be envisaged by the person who intends enhancing the role through their unique ability. The result is that most employees and therefore most businesses perform well below their potential.

Conventional Teamwork versus Unique Teamwork

We must be careful to distinguish between conventional and unique teamwork because they are worlds apart in both vision and capability. Conventional teamwork can mean anything from a team simply sharing a common workload, to dividing work functions between people, even with high value skill sets, but to achieve a 'conventional' team goal – i.e. a goal that is visualised as achievable without the need to draw on the unique ability, innovativeness and entrepreneurial drive of each team member.

The crucial factor requiring unique teamwork is a vision for a goal that would be impossible to achieve with conventional teamwork because it demands so much more. This does not mean that conventional teamwork becomes irrelevant. It still has its place when work does not demand unique ability – and this can be quite often as described in our chapter on impact management. However, unique teamwork presents a team with the opportunity to create bigger goals and achieve bigger results by making use of each team member's unique ability whenever possible, and by seeking ways to create new combinations of this value.

For example, a technology installation team hits a snag on site that will cause a delay in completion that will clearly upset their customer. In conventional teamwork mode, an apology is be made by the operations manager while the team works to rectify the problem. Damage to the client relationship is unavoidable. However, the problem is handled differently in unique teamwork mode. The operations manager whose unique ability is to 'always seek and find opportunity from difficulty', calls the chief technology officer whose unique ability is 'to see technical solutions others don't see'. Together they seek fresh insight into finding a possible solution. They are rewarded. By looking at the problem differently, an opportunity is recognised to introduce some new equipment with a higher specification at the same price, which will also short cut some installation processes. The sales director, whose unique ability is to 'foster very high levels of trust with customers', communicates the upgrade and its benefits to the client. This is achieved, leaving everyone happy.

Unique Teamwork and Elite Teams

The essential difference in an elite team is that it is able to accomplish what other teams would not even attempt. And these accomplishments are made possible only through unique teamwork. This ability is not so much a reflection of 'technical' competence (a basic requirement for any level of employment), as it is a combination of the unique skills and aptitudes that define the members that make up the team. These are not necessarily super talented or educated people, but ordinary people who not only believe they can do extraordinary things, but who get on and do them. Motivated by a clear company vision, a mission for customers, and clear personal goals that drive their success, they become irresistible to customers.

Selection for an Elite Team

While most of us think that we are already eligible for selection in an elite business team because of the skills we have acquired, the truth is that many of us would not qualify – yet. People who aspire to be part of an elite team learn to make choices other people avoid making. They make the choice to work hard in investing in their personal development and its application to their work, to the point at which real impact can be measured... and then work hard to improve it. It is a choice to be true to one's 'inner call' for significance and meaning in the workplace by being the best we can be. It is a call to excellence, that once it is made, begins our journey toward *personal impact*.

Working in an Elite Team

People, who work in an elite team, make choices other people avoid making

In this section we explore the final five *Laws of Noble Enterprise* that, in conjunction with the previous ten laws, empower *ordinary* teams to become *elite* teams:

1. Relationships in an elite team.
2. Leveraging impact.
3. Defending the team.
4. Innovation.
5. Sustainable growth.

Relationships in an Elite Team

As the intrinsic value and impact of products and services is entirely dependent on people, in a global economy there is a new urgency to unlock the competitive edge that people bring to business. Although much good work has been done to better engage employees in their work, there is still a lot more to do to unlock this competitive value. We have already explored the necessity of identifying and deploying unique ability at both an individual and team level to achieve this. However, to do this requires close relationships to be developed between team members, for without knowledge of each other *and* acceptance of each other the unique ability of team members, will almost certainly remain undiscovered.

Beyond Engagement

A close bond is formed between the members of an elite team and develops through four stages. Stage one is an *appreciation* for each other's skill and unique ability. Stage two is the *support* members offer each other because of this appreciation. Stage three is the *integration* of team members' unique ability into unique teamwork. Finally, stage four is the *partnership* that is formed, through which ambitious projects are undertaken. It is this partnership forged by appreciation, support and integration that emboldens the team to take on new and bigger challenges and win.

But before this bonding process between team members can even begin, it is essential to have an atmosphere of trust within the team. This starts by team members valuing each other for who they are as people, not what they can do. This runs contrary to a work culture that does not see the need for good relationships amongst employees as essential to bringing value to the company and its customers. It is an inarguable fact that the hidden talents and aspirations of employees, and the personal confidence needed to express them, can only be developed in a culture where these human characteristics are highly esteemed.

Appreciating Each Other

> *There is urgency to unlock more of the competitive edge people bring to business*

The level of confidence a person has is often the distinguishing factor between a good performance and great performance from them. Because working in an elite team is primarily about performance, it is important that team members help to develop each other's confidence. This is achieved by appreciating and realistically evaluating each other's skill and unique ability by offering input where appropriate. It is the trust that develops between team members that allows this to happen. We must also not forget that by helping each other we are helping ourselves too, because everyone is pursuing the same goal.

Supporting Each Other

The appreciation of the skill and unique ability among members of an elite team is what attracts support for each other. This support is further enhanced by the mutual respect members have for one another, because of their commitment to deliver the value that is demanded of them. This level of support, not usually found in conventional teams, is displayed in a variety of ways, from offering encouragement when needed, to willingly helping correct problems when things go wrong. In a team where mutual support is the norm, no one feels undervalued or disconnected.

Integrating with Each Other

With team members fully appreciating and supporting each other, integration of each other's unique ability into unique teamwork can take place unhindered. This is an exciting time for any team who discovers that they have at their disposal, a new and very powerful capability that was not previously available nor understood. It means that current work goals and targets, now viewed through the lenses of this new capability, can be achieved with a new quality and efficiency, leaving room to explore bigger goals (more about this later).

Partnering Together

Unique teamwork is the result of the tight working bond formed between like-minded people, who have developed the ability and confidence to take on challenges that people working in conventional teams would not consider. It is a partnership formed by applying the eleventh entrepreneurial law – **Build Relationships** (see figure 20 below).

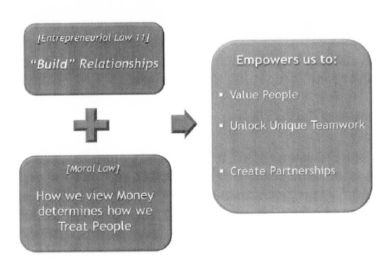

Figure 20
Beyond Engagement is Partnership

Building relationships is not always easy given our differences. However, when we apply the principles being discussed we will be pleasantly surprised at how flexible and willing people are at developing their place in an elite team.

Relationships and Money

How we view Money determines how we Treat People is the moral law attached to how we build relationships in the workplace. Because of the melting pot business creates between the focus on money and relationships (covered in part 2), we need to distinguish between our personal need *for* money, and a *love of money*, to avoid the subtle trap of money consciously or subconsciously controlling us. If it does, we will lose sight of the true value of the people we work with. This will, in turn, restrict how they relate to us, thereby affecting their level of engagement with us, and their performance in our team. Ultimately, this will limit team results.

How we view money is a moral issue we must all face and make a decision on.

Building healthy relationships in a team means:

• Liking yourself and enjoying your own company.

• Building strong relationships with team colleagues.

• Team colleagues wanting *you* to succeed.

• You wanting team colleagues to succeed.

• Influencing organisational relationships outside of your team.

Leveraging Impact

The concept and real value of unique teamwork to a business is incomplete without exploring the leveraging of impact that is possible when team members create synergy, using their unique ability. Synergy is a word full of promise. Its necessity is inspired when a team, facing a goal that is so big that it is beyond their obvious capability, still want to achieve it, and believe they can. To do so, they must now seek new creative ways of combining their respective abilities to achieve the goal. It means exploring opportunities to mix and match their unique skills to accomplish a difficult task, lift value to a customer, or increase efficiency.

To develop synergy, team members must learn to call on and rely on each other, when they know the value required for the job at hand demands the unique ability of a particular person. It means letting someone else take charge of a situation when it is in their realm of expertise.

When big goals are achieved through team synergy, motivation in a team soars, and a new level of passion emerges for a 'team cause' that is built on the team's uniqueness and entrepreneurial drive, that is bigger than the team itself. The team now knows that what they are capable of achieving is well beyond the ability of any single member. It is this new appreciation of each other, and the team, that opens the way to confidently take on new challenges that are considered worthy of the team's capability, and that result in a new identity which the team will want to protect. This leveraging of a team's impact is what grows its value and reputation with customers.

Synergy Explained

Many people confuse synergy with elementary teamwork, which is nothing more than a team leader coordinating people's activity better. Synergy is much more powerful, much more challenging and much more humbling. Synergy is an everyday concept found throughout nature, and in much of what we as humans design and produce, but we rarely see it functioning between people in the workplace on a daily basis. Essentially, it is about leveraging the intrinsic value contained in the different components of something, in order to produce a bigger result than the sum of the value of the components. There are two types of synergy to be considered. The first one is *designed synergy* where expected performance is predetermined and limited by design.

For example, we can see this demonstrated in an internal combustion engine, where each of the many components is pre-designed with a specific purpose in mind. After careful assembly to ensure that each component is correctly connected, the designed power output at the crankshaft can be produced. In *designed synergy* the end goal, which is always the same, is envisioned by the designer, who then designs or seeks to find, parts that fit the whole. Traditional team or organisational design is a bit like this. Predetermined job roles and their outputs are defined by a 'designer', and then people are sought to 'fit' these roles. The best that can be achieved with this approach is conventional team work. Here synergy can be, and is sometimes achieved, but it is limited by the constraints of conventional teamwork which have already been discussed.

The second type of synergy is *creative synergy*. In this case, performance is based on the imaginative responses of a team to challenges — as they occur. Here, team members recognise each other's uniqueness, and then exploit it by exploring and applying the synergies that are possible, in order to overcome a particular challenge or achieve a goal. The difference with *creative synergy* is twofold. Not only is the team in control of their responses and not an external designer, but more importantly, the team is in control of accomplishing what they consider to be their own mission and goal. It provides a team with almost endless value combinations, and a combined capability that takes any business to a new level.

> **'Creative synergy' relies on imaginative responses to overcome big challenges**

For example, the *creative synergy* in the unique teamwork that is displayed by two English Premier League football teams battling it out on the football pitch provides awe inspiring entertainment to fans all over the world, and hours of after match analysis and comment. In a business environment, it is this *creative synergy* that will enable new sales targets to be reached, new innovations to be launched, new efficiencies to be found and new profits to be 'mined' and generated. It is this *creative synergy* in unique teamwork that will set a business apart from its competitors and guarantee its growth.

*

To illustrate the concept, we will continue the narrative of Bailey's Logistics Plc. It is now fifteen months since taking on the new contract for Eagle Star Foods and things could not have gone better. Everyone is delighted. But Bailey's Logistics has a new challenge.

They are in the process of extending the size of their distribution centre to be able to cope with the growth in volume from their growing customer base, but until its completion three months away, they face an almost impossible task – they need to increase the throughput of their existing facility to 115% of its design capacity, and they have to do it now.

The only way this can be achieved is to speed up the throughput without compromising accuracy or safety. This would require reorganising the distribution centre into four six-hour shifts instead of three eight-hour shifts to enable employees to maintain the higher pace demanded of them. Because of the very high standards Bailey's Logistics demands of itself, it is very reluctant to outsource this extra workload to another operator that does not share its values. But keeping it in-house will have an impact not just on deliveries, but also on the planning, administration, logistical backup and maintenance functions that support the deliveries. For the three month duration of the challenge, all distribution centre staff would now have to focus only on the most important aspects of their work, while relying on backup staff to fill in any gaps.

Bob Jones let his organisation make the decision. Could they do it, and did they want to? He received a resounding "yes" from everyone. Keen to show that they were up for the challenge, and to put into practice their training on synergy and unique teamwork, team leaders and their teams set about examining their work routines to see what needed to change to accomplish the goal. Here is a summary of what happened.

1. Extra vehicles and drivers were hired, but the drivers first had to attend and pass the Bailey's Logistics *Customer Impact Course*, which included spending three days with existing drivers on their rounds. Existing drivers were given the task of passing or failing candidates. Four out of ten new drivers hired did not pass and were replaced.

2. The extra staff required to make up the numbers for the added shift, were made up from teams in other departments. A roster system was set up so that everyone in the company had the opportunity to help in the distribution centre – including team leaders. To free staff up to do this, the remaining staff had to look for creative ways of keeping up with their workload. The reality of the mounting pressure, together with their resolve to win, caused their unique skills to come to the fore and closer relationships to be formed. It also enabled their work to be processed quicker. Many new lessons were learned and new confidence was developed, resulting in permanent improvements in many areas.

3. While regular distribution staff took charge of the most important functions of picking orders, driving forklift trucks and cranes, back up staff went into support mode by sorting paperwork and helping drivers check and load their consignments. Everyone kept their eyes on the scoreboard because everyone was committed.

4. They did it. They achieved their goal. The extension was completed and routines went back to normal with new lessons learned. Everyone was given an extra two weeks' leave that year and an extra bonus. Their shares grew in value too.

Applying Synergy

Synergy starts with a goal that is so inspiring and stretching that team members know unless something very special happens between them, there is little chance of achieving it. This is when the twelfth entrepreneurial law, **Practice Unique Teamwork**, is needed because synergy demands practice and experimentation.

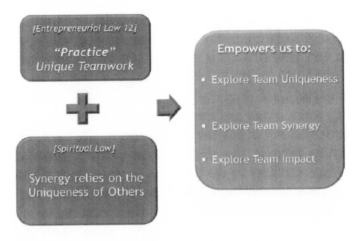

Figure 21
Being a Critically Important part of a much Bigger Picture

Team members must acknowledge that the synergy they desire requires dependence on colleagues who are much better at certain things than they are. This is the difficult part, because it requires humility not be threatened by the strengths of others. This is a problem often found in a team, when one member finds it difficult to make way for another to play their unique role. This becomes a real problem when a team leader believes that no team member has skills they do not possess. The answer lies in the liberating truth of the spiritual law **Synergy relies on the Uniqueness of Others** (see figure 21). When team members know the value of their unique ability to the team, and have the confidence to display it when needed, they are not threatened by anyone with skills they do not have. True leadership is required to start and develop the process of unique teamwork. The skills required to do this are discussed in later chapters.

So why do we not see synergy in practice when our businesses so desperately need it? Here are three reasons worth considering.

1. Team goals are usually not stretching enough.

2. Individuals, including leaders, feel threatened by others being better at certain things than they are.

3. Leaders spend most of their energy and time managing "What *needs* to be achieved" rather than pursuing "What *can* be achieved".

Included in Customer's Strategic Plans

When the collective uniqueness of a team is unleashed in a powerful and coordinated display of synergy directed towards achieving a customer's goal, it is easy to understand how that team would be included in that customer's future plans. After experiencing such high value, the customer won't want to risk inferior value from elsewhere.

It is this *personal impact,* and entrepreneurial drive inherent in unique teamwork, that is able to build and secure the success of a business irrespective of the external market conditions in which it operates. It is these characteristics that will always enable a business to adapt to changing conditions without compromising its standards, and thereby ensuring it will always have customers.

This is the climax of team endeavour and organisational possibility that this book seeks to promote. It is also the gateway to unlocking a 'gold mine' of opportunity and profit hitherto undetected, but available to any business that cares to 'mine' it.

Leveraging impact in a team means:

• Expecting an elite standard of performance within your team.

• Drawing on the unique ability and value of every team member.

• Seeking synergy from team uniqueness.

• Always delivering improved performance.

• Always being included in customers' strategic plans.

Defending the Team

Successful teams have a lot to protect, and the greater the success, the more commitment there is to this protection. Teams that have worked hard to earn their success, and the reputation that comes with it, have been through a rigorous process to understand each other and to explore synergies. They have developed the capability to build the business in which they work, and from this success, generate expanding opportunities in which everyone in the team has a vested interest. A successful team is a powerful unit of capable people who are committed to the business they are building, the customers they serve, and each other. They have something valuable worth defending.

The reverse is also true. Where teams do not achieve anything noteworthy, there is little value worth protecting as a team. In such cases, value to the business and its customers is often fragmented, and interest in the success of the business and its customers is limited to protecting jobs and incomes. With a shrunken interpretation of the purpose for work, the potential for *personal impact* is lost, leaving mediocrity as the winner.

Obstacles to Unity and Performance

Problems emerge when individuals see themselves as more important than the 'community' in which they function. This can apply to any person at any level in a business. And this is made much worse when a leader's career interests are disconnected from the interests of the team. Instead of inspiring their team to participate in a vision everyone can 'own', and whose success is dependent on everyone's unique contributions, the potential for both *personal impact* and personal opportunity for everyone is lost. This happens in business all the time and robs all stakeholders of the potential wealth that can be created.

The thirteenth entrepreneurial law, **Align Aspirations**, empowered by the moral law, **The 'Community' is more important than the Individual**, provides the principles to overcome this problem.

Aligning Aspirations

Many teams are a fragile and delicately balanced alliance between people who are only vaguely committed to their goal. But, when a team experience the synergy and value that comes from unique teamwork, they instinctively become a 'community' with a higher collective interest, because they have something valuable to protect. It is the alignment of aspirations that creates this unity and the strong sense of ownership within a team, and the desire to 'close ranks' when necessary, to ensure and protect success. This merging of aspirations, is the 'glue' that holds the team together to protect its *personal impact*.

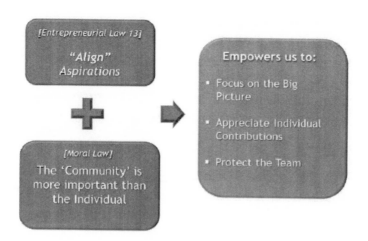

Figure 22
Closing ranks to Protect Success

> *Your team will want to protect you and your unique contribution*

This important step can only be realised when everyone recognises that the team is more important than any single individual. This does not mean that everyone participates equally or provides the same level of value. On the contrary, that is part of the team dynamic that is constantly shifting as people learn and develop, and, as new challenges emerge, is creating new opportunities for people to participate and interact. What it does mean is that the team leader emerges as the 'conductor' of a symphony whose composition is being written as it is being played. While there is always room and need for a 'soloist', it is everyone else in the 'orchestra' that enables the solo piece to be appreciated.

The success of unique teamwork in a business brings a shared confidence to team members where:

1. There is certainty that there is nothing else anyone would like to be doing, and nowhere else they'd like to work.

2. Colleagues' interests are vehemently protected.

3. Team members are not tempted to compare 'their deal' and working conditions with those of other companies.

4. Team members are inspired by their work.

5. Team members know that when the team achieve important goals it is a shared experience.

Innovation

Companies whose employees innovate stay in the driving seat of change and opportunity. Those that do not innovate must rely on spin-off opportunities from companies that do; which means they are not in control of their own destiny, or worse, are on a slide towards obsolescence.

The necessity for ongoing innovation for every business in every sector cannot be overstated; neither can its application to employees and their work. For it is only when innovation is applied by employees in developing their own commercial value, that this same driving force can be extended to their work and its contribution to innovation in the business in which they are engaged. Management consultant Peter Drucker said – *"There is only one competence for the future – innovation and the ability to measure its performance."* Our economic survival is dependent on it.

There is a direct connection between the level of innovation occurring in a business and the level of entrepreneurial drive in its employees. The innovative prowess available to a business from its employees is largely based on how well their unique ability and unique teamwork is being expressed, because it is through these that individual and team brilliance is applied within a business. For the sake of clarity, let's refer to this collective ability and drive of employees to innovate as that business's *Creative Capital*. This creative capital is as important to any business as its financial capital and must be nurtured, protected and invested into the business. Both financial and creative capital must work in tandem to maximise success.

Bringing creative capital to a business is its employees' opportunity to elevate their value and importance to the business. Innovation happens when employees put their creative capital to work to solve new problems not encountered before or to create new value that did not exist before. Interestingly, this fundamental capability within a business to create new ways to drive saleable value up and costs down is never owned by a business, but by its employees. Therefore one of a CEO's most important tasks is to create an environment and culture where creative capital is developed and made available to the business on an ongoing basis. This is no small task, given the challenge of leading a business and the complexity of engaging employees to offer their highest talents.

> *Innovation is the natural outcome of applying unique ability to a problem*

Business leaders must put their employees in the driving seat of creating new value. This does not mean that innovation is an unstructured process because of course it is, but any structure is only to direct the innovative value that employees are freely producing. To do this they must be allowed time to explore their unique value and not have it choked by overwork.

William Rogers of UKRD reflects on the principles he has adopted to encourage innovation in his business. *"Because innovation is key to almost every business and the type of future it will have, it is critical that an internal climate is created in which people can not only propose different things, ideas and approaches but also challenge the present policies and procedures. Challenges are positively encouraged. The 'blame culture' in a business needs to be completely eradicated and an open and constructive dialogue should be the norm. That's down to the culture and working environment. If you get that right, everything else regarding innovation will follow."*

In another example Ian Jones, a consultant, had a client who introduced an innovative model for hiring salespeople in his business. *"This model was designed to break the cycle of 'poaching talent from the competition', which resulted in a small talent pool being circulated but not enlarged. He hired college leavers who had excelled at sport and came from the communities where the CEOs of his prospective customers lived. This profile yielded energetic, enthusiastic extroverts who were not overawed by the decision makers who they would need to work with in selling conversations. This strategy propelled my client to market leader in five years, a position that they still hold. The majority of those new hires are now account directors, each responsible for tens of millions of dollars in annual revenues."*

Developing Creative Capital

We have already determined that a business's creative capital, and therefore its ability to shape its future, resides within its employees. Having said that, we must also realise that because the world around us is in a constant state of flux, it is impossible to keep pace with all the change that is happening. This can leave employees feeling exposed and stressed, and therefore unable to give their best.

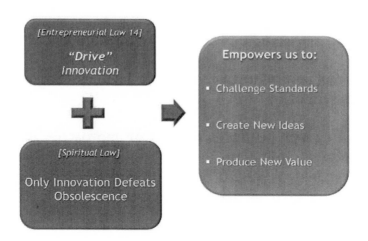

Figure 23
Developing and Maintaining Strategic Value

The fourteenth entrepreneurial law, **Drive Innovation**, encouraged by the spiritual law **Only Innovation Defeats Obsolescence**, is the antidote to this, by helping employees to be more decisive about their contribution to shaping the business's future that reflects more of them. This gives them the confidence that they are part of its future, where their capability is valued and needed, thereby ensuring their own economic viability and growth. But before innovation can take place naturally in a business, the creative capital of its employees must first be developed and deployed. This is achieved by matching the ingenuity of its work force to achieving the strategic interests of the business. How to do this is covered in the chapter on leadership.

Motivation and Application of Creative Capital

When entrepreneurial drive is unlocked within employees, a deep desire to achieve is created. This motivation is refined by goals that are personal and important, making work fulfilling, enjoyable and surprisingly often, even fun. Creative capital is deployed where continuous business improvement is a strategic objective:

1. Setting new standards that competitors are forced to follow.

2. Creating new opportunities for the business that competitors are ignorant of.

3. Creating new products, services or approaches that did not exist before.

Sustainable Growth

We have arrived at the culmination of our journey towards understanding *personal impact*. It is here that all the ideas we have considered, now converge to deliver the often elusive goal sought by every business – sustainable growth. To remind ourselves of the connection between *personal impact* and sustainable growth, let's revisit the definition presented in the introduction. *Personal impact is what employees bring to a business when their collective drive and talent propels it forward to new levels of performance that distinguish it in the minds of customers and competitors.*

> *Employees must reach beyond their current experience*

The growth of any business is always commensurate with the value of the contributions of the employees in it. And it is only through personal impact that the highest individual and team contributions can be guaranteed. This is where the fifteenth entrepreneurial law, ***Reach for Sustainable Growth*** (see figure 24), comes into play. In effect, it means that employees must reach beyond their current experience. This might seem daunting and even unnecessary to employees who limit their capability through their 'job mind-set', but it is not daunting, nor is it considered unnecessary, for people who have trained themselves for the growth that is important to them. It is here that the previous fourteen entrepreneurial, moral and spiritual laws, already embedded deep within their hearts and minds, now stand them in good stead, to make 'reaching beyond current experience' exciting and natural.

Growth and Morality

Sustainable growth is underpinned by true progress, and true progress requires a moral basis. True progress, as defined in this book, is not just about financial advancement, but about making sure that what we do contributes to the well-being of people and society. The moral law that accompanies our reach for sustainable growth, ***Progress is measured by the Good that Results***, means that money is not the only measure of our success, or otherwise, but whether we have contributed to the good of our company, our customers, our society and ourselves. Efforts to grow profits at the expense of peoples' well-being are, and will always be, self-defeating. In the last decade there has been a litany of cases where banks and other large corporate businesses have not only been severely fined for 'taking advantage' of customers, but have almost been destroyed in the process. Some did meet their demise.

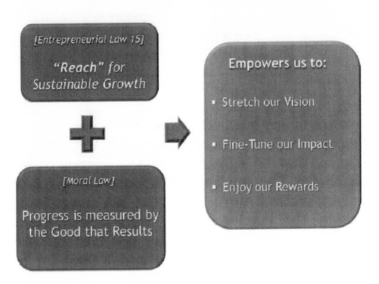

Figure 24
Working for Progress is working for Abundance

Growth without morality has its root in money being an end in itself. In this view, money is seen as the primary answer to life's problems, where enough money and possessions will satisfy us and protect us from the uncertainties of life. This prevailing view is fuelled by fear, and militates against the entrepreneurial, spiritual and moral laws that liberate employees and businesses, and which therefore, also govern sustainable progress. Many companies suffer from this chronic malaise and never achieve sustainable growth. Fear produces a *scarcity* mentality, and this diminishes what people in the business believe can be achieved.

Sustainable growth however, relies on entrepreneurial confidence, which produces an *abundance* mentality in people, who then believe anything is possible. Adopting a moral base to growth protects employee wellbeing and ensures that their entrepreneurial drive is not quenched.

Reaching Beyond Current Experience

Engaging employees in the sustainable growth of a business is only possible where they:

1. Believe in their leaders and their motives.

2. Feel like a stakeholder in their company.

3. Want to defend their company's reputation.

4. Are able to devote a significant portion of time fine-tuning their contribution.

Leading an Elite Team

Leadership inspires vision in others

When the need for entrepreneurial drive is recognised as a strategic imperative to a company's success, it will be built into its operational plans and reward system. Then, when leaders experience the transformation that it brings to their personal work and value to the business, they will want to introduce the principles into the culture of their teams. This will result in teams never being distracted from their customer centric missions.

In this section we explore seven sequential leadership imperatives to help leaders ensure this happens:

1. Create and convey vision
2. Be an inspiration
3. Create a positive environment
4. Win trust
5. Communicate effectively
6. Mentor performance
7. Drive strategy

Step 1: Create & Convey Vision

A business vision must be personal for everyone who must implement it. Only when people... 'taste' it... and 'feel' it... will they personalise it and... 'want' it. This is the starting point of connecting employees and their potential *personal impact* to a business's vision.

> *Only when the team... 'taste' it... and 'feel it' ... will they personalise it and... 'want it'*

In many companies it is simply assumed that somehow everyone 'gets the vision' and 'buys into it', or worse, that it is not important that everyone is behind it as long as the executive team are. When this happens it is not uncommon for the company head to be the only visionary. The executive team become the implementers of the vision, while operational teams go about their daily jobs with no real connection to the business or its vision and purpose. Result 1 and 2 in figure 25 represent two possible consequences to this approach. With no vision or an indistinct one, team leaders spend the majority of their time 'managing' (not leading) their teams. This absorbs valuable time and energy. In this scenario *personal impact* is not possible.

Entrepreneurial drive in a team context introduces vision sharing without affecting organisational structure and authority. This standard gives *everyone* an opportunity to be a visionary by visualising where and how they can apply their talent to create unique *personal impact* in the context of their role. Team leaders use the company's vision to produce a *team vision* and team members use the team vision to produce a *personal vision*. Result 3 on the next page shows how this can work to create an entirely new result for a business.

Taking Responsibility

Because a leader is responsible for the results their organisation or team produce... good or bad, influencing the way their people *think* and *act* is their responsibility. This is the essence of leadership.

For many leaders, helping their team members see new possibilities and make the shift to *personal impact* requires a real step change in the way they lead their people and sometimes even a step change in their own performance.

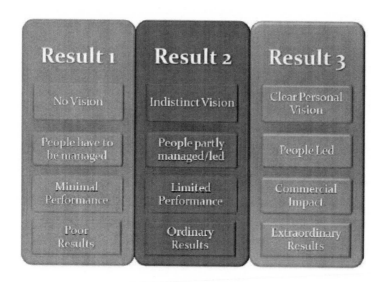

Figure 25

So, to be confident of achieving the results that will bear their name, it is vital that a leader understands how to lift the thinking and performance standards of their team. To permanently change the way employees think about their performance requires that it must first be important enough to them to do so (and money is never a sustainable motivator). So here is the principle that unlocks the process.

What a business requires to distinguish <u>itself</u> and thrive – can only be provided by the people in the business – when <u>they</u> distinguish themselves and thrive.

And leadership is the key to connecting the 'distinguishing and thriving of a business' with the 'distinguishing and thriving' of its employees. This is the umbilical cord that ensures the highest interests of the company, its customers and employees are met. A good leader understands that team members not only *need* to be part of something significant, but deep down they also *want* to be part of something significant even if they don't verbalise it. Involving the team in scripting the team vision and then facilitating the process whereby members write their personal vision, will energise members on their journey to create *personal impact*. This is as much a part of shaping a business as shaping its strategy... and just as important, because the accomplishment of a company's vision is governed by its importance to the employees tasked with its fulfilment.

A business will stall without a vision that challenges employees' aspirations. Vision enables employees to *see* long terms results (for the business and themselves), *and* be sure of them *before* they are actually achieved. It enables them to see the future shape of things, and their part in it. If it's not personal it's not a vision. This is what will motivate everyone through the most difficult times that are sure to come.

Margaret Bennett, managing director for Professional Provident Society in Namibia, said after a training course on developing personal impact: *"I can now understand how my beliefs and personal values can be drawn into, and actually complement, my career life. It gave me confidence that yes, my personal goals can be combined with the company goals, my personal passions can become part of my career passions and I am not so aware of when trying to combine the two. In all my previous jobs I was forced to be me when I am off duty and to be someone else in the workplace. Now, I can actually 'own' my workplace and make it my 'passionate playpen'."*

Leading the Way

William Rogers of UKRD says: *"I have always believed that as long as you have appointed the right people in the right place, you need to get out of the way and encourage them to do their jobs in their own way with the maximum authority and autonomy. Set out the strategic objectives by all means, communicate the messages with clarity, deliver a vision for the business but, in the end, it'll come down to how well your key team members perform as well as the wider company group and for them to do that, you need to genuinely engage them in the business and not pay lip service to that as a concept. Further, I think it's really important to be as approachable as possible, so that the usual and all too frequently erected barriers between team and management are comprehensively demolished."*

Step 2: Be an Inspiration

Inspiration is the stimulus from a leader that awakens a team to possibilities they could not see before, but that the leader clearly does see, believe in and want. The components of inspiration that are experienced by team members are *vision, belief* and *desire*. One component leads to the other, and inspiration is the combination of all three. It starts when a leader shares new possibilities with their team. At this stage they exist only as ideas in the minds of the team, but as the leader's belief is observed, they start to become believable for the team. As their belief develops, certainty sets in and the possibilities now become real, though they are yet to be achieved. Then desire takes over, making inspiration tangible within the team.

> *Inspiration is the tangible effect a leader has on the actions of their team*

This inspiration which is alive in a leader is transferred to the team, enabling them to take on the vision and make it their own, and thereby wanting what the leader wants. But leader inspiration must be constant to ensure team enthusiasm – a significant but critical challenge for any leader. If enthusiasm is lost, team effort can be reduced to the ordinariness of work, and the vision reduced to dried ink on a page. Leader inspiration is what provides the motivating environment in which team entrepreneurial drive can thrive.

But what, you might ask, are the practical benefits of inspiration to performance and profitability? In a business that relies only on the quality and attention to detail of their employees' work, inspiration is not necessarily required, only a good work ethic. However, if a business relies on employees to consistently 'break new ground' with service levels, finding new customers or product and process innovation, then leader and team inspiration is the life-blood of its strategy's execution and financial future.

So, how does a leader know if they are inspiring their team or not? When people in a team *voluntarily* do things *beyond expectations* that is a good sign that inspiration is tangible. However, if it has been a while since the team voluntarily did anything surprising, then it is probably time to rethink the effectiveness of leader inspiration.

Step 3: Create a Positive Environment

Inspiration needs a positive environment in which to thrive. Creating a positive environment is the leader's strategy to protect the tangible effect of their inspiration on the people they lead. It is done by setting a high standard for *thoughts, words* and *actions* to create the culture in which the mission is pursued and achieved.

> *A good leader has a*
> *positive attitude, especially in a crisis*

A positive environment does not necessarily mean an easy environment. On the contrary, the tougher the mission is, the tougher the environment in which it is executed. Elite sports and military teams do not operate in easy environments, but the most difficult environments. It is no different for elite business teams. No leader has to work hard at creating a positive environment at a party or pub evening, but they do when their team is 'feeling the heat'. To counter difficult circumstances when they emerge, a leader must ensure that they control their thoughts, and not be distracted from their mission, and then make these thoughts 'visible' to the team through their words and actions.

This is the toughest aspect of the leader's role — keeping faith and being positive when things get difficult. This is when they are tempted to ask themselves "Is it worth it?", "Was the goal not too high to start with?" Leaders know that the higher their aspirations, the harder it is to achieve them... but can easily forget that this is equally true, but even more difficult, for those they lead.

Examples abound in professional sport and in history, where tight situations have been turned around because a leader refused to give up. It is this very characteristic that separates the elite leader from the ordinary leader. The ordinary leader has a limited capacity to resist 'opposition' (from whatever quarter), while the elite leader refuses to allow difficulties to get in the way and undermine their inspiration. They do this by creating a positive environment. In fact, the elite leader uses difficulties as the best opportunity to demonstrate how strongly they believe in what they are doing.

The hallmark of a good leader is the ability to lead with a positive attitude... especially in a crisis... or better still, to avoid one. How then does the leader consistently create a positive and uplifting work environment that will be decisive in achieving an elite mission?

Step 4: Win Trust

Trust is the relational bond between a leader and team. It unlocks the mutual confidence necessary between members that merges their competence and commitment to achieving their goal. When trust is high almost anything can be achieved, but when trust breaks down, no amount of competence can rescue commitment to the goal, making failure certain. Trust is simply that important.

> *When trust is high almost anything can be achieved...trust is that important.*

It is the magnitude of the shared goal (what is at stake), and the level of competence and commitment required to achieve it, that determines the level of trust necessary between people. The bigger the goal, the more trust is required from the team and therefore the more 'personal' trust becomes. For example, highly paid professional sports teams develop high levels of mutual trust in each other's competence and competitive commitment to win championships. Special Forces personal in the military literally trust their lives on the competence and commitment of their comrades, when they take on the high risk operations they are trained to carry out.

Building High Levels of Trust

For a leader, once the mission to impact customers has been defined, the focus inside the team, like a sports coach, is on nurturing and developing the unique skill and aptitude of each team member.

Because the demands made on elite business teams requires high levels of trust, it is logical for a leader to ask themselves which comes first – their trust in their team, or their team proving they can be trusted. But when we remember that peoples' highest contributions can only be inspired and not forced, leaders are challenged to make the first move in winning the trust of their team to show how trust is built. This takes a great belief in peoples' innate ability, even when it is not outwardly demonstrated at first. Building trust is a process whereby trust must first be shown to those who need to be trusted. It is a process that must be believed in, and that requires commitment, as does any approach to performance improvement.

Tristan Hunkin tells his story that illustrates how trust is developed. *"A couple of years ago my father died – shortly before the Sunday Times Best Companies To Work For ceremony in London, where UKRD was nominated. I was gutted not to be able to attend – and overwhelmed when my phone rang on the evening itself. The Group Programme Director, one of four of the most senior people in the organisation, had called so that I could listen to the top ten countdown being read. When UKRD was named as the winner he took the phone up on the stage with him, so he could pass me around and speak to colleagues who were there. It was a very special moment – and something that he didn't need to do. A couple of days later, at the weekend, he called again and asked if he could come over. He sat in my lounge and chatted to me about what had happened on the night, including all the gossip that I had missed out on. He showed me videos and photos from the event – and checked that I was OK."*

Step 5: Communicate Effectively

The leader of an elite team must be confident that their highest intentions will always be understood. They must ensure there is no dilution of their message, and therefore no soft underbelly to team plans. This is one of their strengths.

> *Communication determines the spirit and accuracy of how things get done in a team*

With a high level of trust already in place, communication is now the vehicle that facilitates both the spirit and accuracy of how things get done. There must be complete consistency between what is said, how it is said and the actions that support communication. This makes it much more than a set of verbal instructions. Communication now becomes a demonstration of *who* the leader is as a person. This helps to convey not only their strategies and plans, but their inspirational ideas, ideals, standards and values they consider necessary to achieve their mission.

There are no contradictions in their message as the team listens with their ears, their eyes and their hearts. Because of this transparency and honesty from the team leader, everyone in the team takes full ownership of the mission and its goals, bending over backwards to achieve them, while helping colleagues do the same.

In an elite team everyone is respected for who they are and what they bring to the team. If team members are not sure of something, they have the confidence to ask without fear of rebuke. Team members are tuned into the opportunities and threats of their mission and are often in a position to make observations that the leader cannot make. These observations are always welcome.

Good communication by a leader means they are able to influence their team by inspiring growth, and connecting this to the thinking, behaviour and performance required of their team. This is how a leader knows they are not stagnating.

But teams also reflect poor leadership. While good leaders take personal responsibility for how 'their' team is doing, poor leaders don't. This is a sign that growth and change is not happening, with results probably demonstrating this to be the case.

Step 6: Mentor Performance

Leading an elite team also means being the team coach. There are two reasons why this is necessary. Firstly, as an elite team is defined by its performance, the entire team must engage itself in learning from its experiences and applying this to continually tweak performance. The role of team leader is to coordinate this and help fuse it into a seamless learning experience. Secondly, a team leader must ensure that team performance is commensurate with the pace of change demanded of it by the business it serves. Increased focus on innovation and new complex business challenges require ongoing mentoring to keep the team relevant and competitive.

Both these challenges require constant input into the team by the leader. If this is not done, then the value of their leadership to their team and to the business will stagnate. When stagnation occurs, it also causes development of the team to lag. Time that might have been used to bring impact to the business is taken to 'catch up'. The danger, of course, is that when stagnation becomes endemic in a team or organisation, and it is no longer recognised, it enters hazardous territory. This is a common occurrence in businesses that have allowed work output to trump impact. More and more companies are falling victim to this problem as financial insecurity and competitive pressure increase, and staff numbers are cut to reduce costs. This leaves more work to be accomplished with fewer people.

Work Output versus Impact

> *When stagnation becomes endemic
> in an organisation, it is no longer recognised*

One of the greatest challenges of a team leader is to manage the balance between work output and impact, as both are important. To do so a leader must be free to lead and not be overwhelmed by work load. This applies to the team too. Applying learning to keep a team's value fresh is detailed work that can only happen at a team level, involving everyone in the team.

It is imperative, then, that work load pressure is controlled so that it does not nullify this effort. The only way a leader can resist extraneous work load pressure, is to be confident of the *personal impact* delivered within their team. Paying close attention to their *impact management* deals with this dilemma.

Step 7: Drive Strategy

Driving a business's strategy is the key role of a leader at any level and is the key measure of their success. This means bringing 'life' to its execution.

> *Execution without entrepreneurial drive is ineffectual and lifeless*

Although it is a chief executive's role to create and drive a business's strategy from the top of an organisation, it is only the entrepreneurial dynamism of leaders and their teams at every level that can transform it into a day to day customer experience. Any execution without the entrepreneurial drive of committed employees is ineffectual and lifeless, diluting the chief executive's vision for the business.

We have now come full circle from the question first asked in the introduction to the book. *"How much of the 'grand vision' that permeates the mind of a business leader gets reduced to a 'budget' in the mind of managers, a 'task' in the mind of staff members, and an 'indifferent experience' for customers... deflecting revenue and profits to competitors?"*

We should now have a better understanding of how vital it is for companies to do everything in their power to encourage and develop entrepreneurial drive in their employees, and the importance of team leadership in bringing this about.

Questions to consider

• Unique teamwork opens new doors to team impact. How important is it in your organisation to explore and even invest in new approaches to employee effectiveness?

• Would the notion of 'Elite Teams' better engage employees in your company?

• How well do you think team leaders in your organisation display the seven leadership imperatives just described?

Part 6

Everyone Wins!

In conclusion I would like to review four areas which are directly and positively impacted by employee entrepreneurial drive. These four areas also show the broader implications of this approach to business.

More Cash, less Fuss

A business must always be generating cash, and lots of it. There is nothing more disheartening than working in a cash-strapped business that is also devoid of entrepreneurial drive. There is so much that needs doing but no money to do it with. The pressure that mounts on the management team that is redirected downwards to everyone else, makes things go from bad to worse.

Businesses with employees that exude entrepreneurial drive generate more cash than businesses that don't. It is their underlying enthusiasm, creativity, skill and perseverance that brings a business plan to life and cash into the bank. This book explores the reasons why this is so. What a huge difference this makes for the lives of executives, managers, staff and investors. Work becomes exciting, fulfilling and rewarding for everyone.

In addition, where more capital is required to fund a growing business, investors will be more attracted to one that has a strong entrepreneurial drive than to one that doesn't.

Corporate Community

For a business to have 'heart' it must have a sense of community amongst employees. Having a purpose which is bigger than individuals and teams, yet allows full expression of both, means synergy can be developed through an entire organisation. Individuals become champions within a team; teams become champions with the organisation; the organisation becomes a champion in the marketplace.

Corporate community avoids the blunder of buying or selling a company without taking into consideration the commitment of the people in it. It is inspired by:

1. Heritage – protecting the reputation and achievements of the organisation.

2. Pride – a sense of privilege in creating history.

3. Vision – employees being part of a cause bigger than themselves.

4. Ethics and values – a culture of principle, truth and decency.

5. Belonging – being part of a community with a shared future.

Ricky Kujawa, president and founder member of International Collaborative Consultancy Cooperative, illustrates this through an interesting story of a Turkish bank that has grown rapidly while managing to reduce its cost ratios. *"Top management lead from the front, visiting regions and branches regularly and ensuring that they speak 1-to-1 with each member of staff during their visit. The bank has become adept at forward thinking and anticipative leadership. The corporate colour is green. More than one member of staff told me 'if you cut me I will bleed green.' Perhaps more impressive was the choice of song which summed up how some staff felt about working there. Based on a folk tune, they said, 'If you didn't exist I would have to invent you.'"*

Impact on Share Price

It is my belief that in the context of increasing global financial uncertainty, the survival, growth and sustainability of every business is boosted or restricted by the strength or weakness of the entrepreneurial drive within its management team and organisation. To that end a measurement tool has been created to measure the entrepreneurial drive and its application by employees in a business, termed its *Commercial Impact Index*. The supposition is, that the higher the value of the index... the greater the profit expectations... and the more certainty there is of achieving them. This measure can be applied to both private companies and listed ones.

If this assumption proves correct, then it follows that a point can be reached where the commercial impact delivered by employees in a company is so strong, that growth in profits becomes certain and predictable. The possibility of a practical index that links the personal impact of managers and employees directly to predictable future profitability would introduce a new factor that helps lift investor confidence and company share value.

The question of people and listed share prices has already been asked in different ways. *"So when people ask 'is Human Capital actively used in valuing stocks today' the answer is both 'yes' and 'no'. No, I never see an explicit value put on any parts of Human Capital and it is never capitalised on the balance sheet. But 'yes', people issues matters a lot when investors, analysts and companies assess the market value of a company."* (Morten Kamp Andersen)

"Market sentiment refers to the psychology of market participants, individually and collectively. This is perhaps the most vexing category because we know it matters critically, but we are only beginning to understand it." (Davis Harper – Investopedia Website)

"There have been many studies that have documented long-term historical phenomena in securities markets that contradict the efficient market hypothesis and cannot be captured plausibly in models based on perfect investor rationality." (Davis Harper – Investopedia Website)

Business libraries are awash with many useful books that attempt to explain and measure the effect of people on business performance. There are also many useful measuring tools available that go some way in addressing this subject. However, the fact that there is still no accepted universal measure, and in particular, nothing that can be used by investors in assessing the value of a company's human capital, demonstrates that the direct link between how people think and act in a business and the results they produce, is yet to be measured and proven. When it is proven, it will form the basis for a dramatic reappraisal on how investors view companies, and in particular listed companies, and how employees are measured, trained and rewarded.

Impact on Society

The prosperity of a society is a reflection of the prosperity of the businesses in it, and the value employees who work in those businesses, bring to them. More importantly, the levels of prosperity in a society are an indication of how people are thinking and acting to bring change and growth to their lives. A lack of prosperity reflects not just a lack of resources, but a lack of will and hope too.

When the principles presented in this book become rooted in people, they become life changing and permanent. Entrepreneurial drive produces creative and positive people who do not shy away from challenge, but are drawn to it. The same energy and enthusiasm they apply in the workplace to create financial prosperity, is also applied to other areas of their lives, including the way they bring up their children. Children are brought up to take responsibility for their future and not to rely on the state. They are taught to develop themselves by studying hard and to play hard too.

Entrepreneurial drive brings a contagious optimism which rubs off on other people. It encourages them to see beyond their current circumstances and to step out and make the most of their life and its opportunities. It stimulates people to dig deep to find and develop their own personal impact and discover the profound fulfillment that this brings to their work life.

Commercial Impact Index

Employee Impact on Company Earning Power

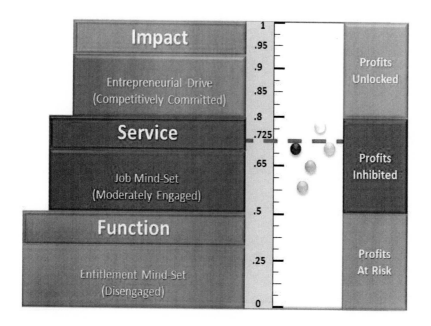

www.CommercialImpactIndex.com

www.lovemondays.global

Lightning Source UK Ltd.
Milton Keynes UK
UKOW04f0618210116

266837UK00002B/43/P